If I Am Not
For Myself...

THE FREE PRESS
A Division of Macmillan, Inc.
New York

Maxwell Macmillan Canada
Toronto

Maxwell Macmillan International
New York Oxford Singapore Sydney

If I Am Not For Myself...

THE
LIBERAL BETRAYAL
OF THE JEWS

Ruth R. Wisse

The Free Press
A Division of Simon & Schuster
1230 Avenue of the Americas
New York, NY 10020

The Free Press and colophon are trademarks
of Simon & Schuster Inc.

Manufactured in the United States of America

10 9 8 7 6 5 4 3

Library of Congress Cataloging-In-Publication Data

Wisse, Ruth R.
        If I am not for myself— :the liberal betrayal of the jews / Ruth R. Wisse.
               p.   cm.
        Includes bibliographical references.
        ISBN: 978-0-7432-2961-6
        1.   Jews—Politics and government. 2. Liberalism. 3. Right and
        Left (Political science) 4. Antisemitism. 5. Israel—Politics and
        Government. 6. Israel and the diaspora. 7. Imaginary letters.
        I.   Titles.
        DS143.W65   1992   P2-22812
        305.892'4—dc20   CIP

For information regarding special discounts for bulk purchases, please contact Simon
& Schuster Special Sales at 1-800-456-6789 or business@simonandschuster.com

To Rina and Itzhak Zamir and their children
who gave us a home in Israel

Contents

Preface

Belief in progress is one of the most cherished assumptions of the modern age. How can we help believing in human improvement when through their intelligence and perseverence people have flown to the moon, doubled life expectancy, and made the desert bloom with new species of fruit and flower? Since our European ancestors began to recognize themselves as the masters of their fate, they taught us to be positive and hopeful about the future and to have faith in the progressive betterment of all the world. In America, people were even granted the right to the "pursuit of happiness."

The fate of modern Jews stands in sharpest contradiction to this modern faith. Although Jews were among the most enthusiastic champions of the idea of progess, contributing as individuals to the advancement of knowledge and culture, and as a society to the furtherance of democracy and freedom, they were singled out as victims of the most barbaric crime in recorded history—and within the very culture that had claimed highest credit for self-advancement. Moreover, far from curbing Jew-hatred, the success of Nazi Germany in destroying the Jewish communities of Europe encouraged

Israel's Arab antagonists to develop a new and improved anti-Semitism as the cornerstone of their own emerging modern nationalist ideology. Anyone who bothers to trace the progress of anti-Semitism in Europe from the birth of the idea in the 1870s to the murder of the Jews in the 1940s will marvel at the greater speed with which Arab propaganda has discredited the moral standing of the Jewish state since the introduction of the Zionist-racist equation at the United Nations in the 1970s. This book tries in part to assess these Arab gains.

The nature of anti-Semitism makes it impossible to believe in the progressive improvement of humankind without obscuring the evidence of the Jews. It selects the Jews because despite their immense image they are a very tiny people, ensuring their political isolation, their progressive demoralization, and—if the historical pattern holds—their eventual decimation. This unilateral aggression against an unequal enemy challenges the deepest desires of people in democratic countries for a life free of enmity and strife. No one is grateful to the Jews for being reminded of the reality of hatred. Given the asymmetry between the hunter and his prey, it is easier to resent the Jews than to oppose the anti-Semites.

Liberalism may have been the kindly offspring of Christianity in Europe, but anti-Semitism was its nastier stepchild, and the struggle between these two impulses continues in the modern world. Just as Christianity failed to live up to its own teachings in its treatment of the Jews, so, too, the failure of liberalism is most evident in its betrayal of the Jews to the will of their enemies. Many good people find it psychologically and politically necessary to abandon the Jews to their fate so that they may preserve their easy optimism; if they can then blame the Jews for incurring such hostility, they can assuage their conscience at the same time.

A great deal has already been written about anti-Semitism's selection of the Jews as a scapegoat and political target. This book explores what I think is the more critical problem in democratic society, the way liberalism joins in discrediting the Jews to avoid having to come to their defense.

Because I, too, would have preferred to be hopeful about human progress, I found it very discouraging to write this book. I believe the French Jewish intellectual Alain Finkiel-kraut, speaking for all who attempt it, said, "There is nothing more humiliating than to have to defend the truth." To offset the humiliation, I tried to create for myself a literary atmosphere of national and personal dignity in the epistolary fiction of a woman and a man who love and respect one another. Through these two voices of Jewish experience—the woman in North America and the man who has moved with his family to Israel—I intended to project the unity of the Jewish people despite the circumstances keeping them apart. As I proceeded, however, and the dangers these two Jews faced in common became so much more exigent to me than the problems they faced individually, I found myself eliminating more and more of the epistolary scaffolding, leaving only the bare frame of a prologue and an epilogue. Some readers may feel that this artifice ought to have been eliminated entirely, especially since the concluding reflections on love and loyalty have not been sufficiently prepared for in the unfolding fictional story of the friendship between the correspondents. I sympathize with these objections on artistic grounds and I worry lest the coda, instead of bringing the moral argument of the book to its fullest expression, offend some otherwise sympathetic readers. Nevertheless, I have retained the epistolary framework.

As it happens, the two books that set the terms for this one—Moses Hess's *Rome and Jerusalem* and Hillel Halkin's *Letters to an American Jewish Friend*—are both in epistolary form, perhaps only coincidentally or perhaps because there is something in their Zionist passion that generates this particular combination of intimate reflection and public disclosure. Like theirs, my book also assumes that responsible politics grows from the experience of friendship and family, which is why the personal form may suit the discussion of politics. There is a tendency on the part of the polemicist to deny the complicating features of human behavior for the sake of a clearer argument. Our admission of human complexities into political debate guards against at least the worst dangers of philosophic abstraction that have done so much damage to Western civilization in the name of prescribing its improvement.

It is harder to account for my choice of an unconsummated love to characterize the bond between Jews in Israel and those outside it. While I had in mind no strict political parable, I did want to suggest that because of the unequal burden of defense that is shouldered by the Jews of Israel, ties between the physical defenders of the country and those Jews who live among generously democratic neighbors cannot honestly be described in the hitherto preferred terms of a marriage or an equal partnership. A great sense of anguish divides the Jewish citizens of Israel and those who wish it well from outside its borders. The longer the Arab war against the Jewish state continues, and Arab propaganda tries to drive a wedge between tolerable Jews and wretched Zionists, the harder it will be to maintain mutual love in an unbalanced association.

As part of this tension, I wanted also to explore the contrast in attitudes to love and loyalty between the traditional religiously inspired determination to contain evil and the modern idea that men and women should be liberated from their civilizing constraints. One day the rabbi of my synagogue told this joke: When Moses came down from Sinai with the Ten Commandments, he announced that he had good news and bad news. "The good news—I kept Him down to ten. The bad news—adultery stays." In the congregation's explosion of laughter I found my subject, the connecting dramatic link between moral courage in personal life and in politics.

This book is dedicated to my cousins Itzhak and Rina Zamir and to their children Yoram, Yonatan, and Rachel, who gave us a home in Israel in every sense. The decisions of parents determined their residence in Israel, ours in Canada, alloting to them the heavier task of securing a home for all Jews who may want or need it. Their spirit of hospitality is Zionism incarnate.

I feel no less thankful to Neal Kozodoy, who gave me a home in *Commentary*. I am one of those many readers for whom the advertisement that once ran in the magazine, "In the name of sanity, send me *Commentary*," is literally true, as no publication ever came closer to my sense of the world or gave me so much hope for it. I thank its editors Norman

Podhoretz and Neal Kozodoy for having seen fit to publish some of this book and for the improvements they made to it. I am also very grateful to the publisher of *The New Republic*, Martin Peretz, and to its editors for their insightful help with the sections that first appeared in their magazine.

To Adam Bellow, my editor at The Free Press, my heartfelt thanks for having urged me to turn a collection of letters into a book, and for encouraging me through every step of the process. Glen Hartley's support for this project was decisive; I am most fortunate to have him for an agent.

When it comes to thanking my husband and children for the encouragement that allowed me to write this book, I see the image of my not-at-all-primitive mother spitting *tfoo! tfoo! tfoo!* to ward off the evil eye. I trust that Len, who accompanied me to the Sinai, knows how my ideas of love and friendship were formed. Billy, Jacob, and Abby are always in my thoughts; they are the best reason I know for championing the Jews. Having read the manuscript, each of them—Billy in Los Angeles, Jacob in New York, Abby in Jerusalem—would have wanted it slightly altered, but some of their suggestions were beyond my power to adopt. I hope they are not disappointed.

Letter to a New Israeli

Dear B,

Unhappy as I am that so close a friend is gone, I cannot scold you for leaving. You've done what I think is right, a word that still carries full weight with you and me. I know how much you love Jerusalem. You've told me what a good job awaits you at the university and that you've shipped over a microwave oven for your new apartment, something your wife never enjoyed here. I also know that your sons will soon be serving in the army, how you will writhe in the toils of the Israeli bureaucracy, what a burden of problems you assume as an immigrant. I take you at your word when you say that you have left Canada for Israel only because you want to, but a hero may well be one whose desires happen to coincide with the national imperative.

You may be right that the Jews are, and will remain, a

people united in dispersion. Moored as I am in the city you left, I have every incentive to trust the course of my life. But a Jew within our dispersed people may also be under a particular obligation to know where he is most needed, and if he acts on that knowledge he makes us proud, if also lonelier.

Before you try to squirm out of this stentorian rhetoric about pride and heroism with some wisecrack, let me anticipate your discomfort. Mona Richman, Eliza's sister-in-law, does not share my admiration for your move. By my calculation, at just about the time you were passing through El Al security at Mirabel Airport forty-eight hours ago (no doubt impressing the agents with your elegant Hebrew), I was sitting beside this woman at the *shiva* for Eliza's mother. Mona was my schoolmate through grades one to seven at the *Folkschule*, a girl who never let on how smart she really was. After we had caught up with old times, she became my guide to the Richman family, beginning with the oldest son, Mark, a volunteer in the Israeli army, at present home on compassionate leave. Eliza hoped that he would come back into the family business, but the boy had just let his parents know that when he finished his army service he intended to study electrical engineering at the Technion then settle right there, in Haifa. Mona described the boy as clever and popular, and his good looks I could confirm. "I don't understand," she confided to me, "I thought only losers go to Israel nowadays."

Isn't that a breathtaking formulation? What a treasure of received ideas in this woman's "nowadays." A truly up-to-date Jew, active in the synagogue and in United Israel Appeal, she acknowledges that the Zionist impulse was once creditable, that the Richmans' son and you, my dear loser, would have merited her respect in bygone days. Maybe she retains images of the pioneering one-armed Joseph Trumpeldor on his horse, kibbutzniks raising water towers and draining the Hula swamps, haloed David Ben-Gurion proclaiming the birth of the Jewish state under Theodor Herzl's majestic portrait. After all, she and I once stood side by side in our blue-and-white school choir, piping out Zionist chestnuts. When her little soprano voice trilled "Who will build, will build a house in Tel Aviv? Who will plant, will plant a vineyard in Tel Hai?" she too must have shivered as the boys boomed their answer in voices just beginning to crack, "We the pioneers, will build Tel Aviv. We, the halutzim, will cultivate Tel Hai." Her "nowadays" concedes that people of strength and ambition did once go to Israel, or would have been credited with strength and ambition for determining to live there. Had you gone East then, Mona Richman would have been at the dock, waving the Jewish flag.

You know, I actually remember how that was. In 1949 we drove to Quebec City to see my brother off on the S.S. Tabinta. All year long his Zionist group had met in our living room to work out the details of their trip and to hammer out a common ideology. Their arguments were so fierce I was convinced the Arabs stood no chance. My brother was a moderate, an idealist without portfolio, but the two dozen others who gathered at our house seemed to be setting off on holy missions of their own rich invention. When Joe E., the Communist, spoke about shaping the kibbutz it reminded me of the way he drove his motorcycle: loud, fast, and recklessly. Davy F., smiling sweetly as if his egalitarian vision had already been realized on earth, could with his gentleness persuade an elephant to get up and dance. Tanis, a law student, opposed the agrarian romanticism of the group, insisting that they ought to be founding an urban commune. Without sponsors and at no one's urging, they were off in the first flush of statehood to demonstrate their allegiance to Israel through a long summer's volunteer work on a kibbutz and to pledge their immigration as settlers in the years ahead.

They were so fervent, so glamorous. Their collective departure was the boldest thing I had ever known. I kept beside my bed a snapshot of my brother in a trenchcoat, against the rail of the ship, and turning toward it each morning the way pious Jews turn eastward in prayer, I pledged my own ascent. It was a curse to be five years younger than their eighteen, unable to master the terms of discussion or to join in defending the homeland.

Still, I was not without a small share in that burst of glory. It was my final year at the *Folkschule* before entering high school, and if we couldn't go overseas to help secure the land, at least we were busy securing the myth. The same spring my brother left for Israel our class mounted the most ambitious production the school had ever seen, a full-length drama that we students conceived, wrote, and staged by ourselves. Act 1 was silent. Through a series of frozen tableaux we showed the gradual transformation of broken refugees into illegal immigrants defying the British blockade. Figures dashed to the ground at the start became figures who kissed the ground at the end. Act 2 was a domestic scene in the kitchen of a Canadian Jewish home. The oldest son informs his parents

Prologue: Letter to a New Israeli

that he is leaving for Palestine to throw in his lot with the builders of the new nation. (Lest you see my influence in this, you should know that the older sister of one of my classmates was already a member of kibbutz Eyn Hashofet near the Galilee.) In Act 3, which took a month to research, we reenacted the United Nations debate over the partition plan for Palestine. During the fateful roll call our own hearts stopped every time the girl playing the delegate from Uruguay paused before delivering her decisive yes. Act 4 was the inevitable siege, a Jewish settlement fighting off Arab attack in order to ensure for the nation a different future from what it had known in the past.

We were your ordinary rowdy kids: a boy gashed his head on an overhead pipe during rehearsals, and a girl forefeited her part for tickling the American delegate with a curtain rod during his key UN speech. But look what sure instincts we had. Did we know what we were doing when we dressed everyone in black for the opening act's heavy, static representation of the European past and everyone in white for the noisy, battling finish? How about our balancing of the family sitting around the table in Act 2 with the Family of Man around the table in Act 3? Did we realize the depth of the Jewish yearning for acceptance when, changing scenes, we pulled the little table of the Jewish kitchen into the bigger circle of the United Nations? I'm struck especially by the ensemble concept of the script. There were no leading roles. Most of the play had all of us together on stage (which was also what made us so frisky). To perform the drama of modern Israel you had to draw everyone into the action, because that was how we felt, united as a people, having been joined against our will in destruction, now willingly united to claim our right to live.

In all these aspects the script wrote itself, pronouncing our assurance that we had emerged from darkness into light, from slavery to freedom. We were equally certain that this reversal of our national fate required our participation. Jewish youngsters—at least one in a family—would have to leave the warmth of their Canadian kitchen to help in the ongoing struggle. My brother in his actions, my class in its representation of his actions, felt the same sense of urgency.

Note why we had to go: to fight off the Arab attack. In Act 3 the United Nations confirmed our right to exist as a people on its national soil, but in Act 4 the Arabs continued to deny that right. The theoretical framework of partition collapsed under the real opposition of the Arabs. The Jews would not be granted historical recompense after all but would have to fight for their land the way they once lost it, by military force. The Jewish settlement had to defend itself, to defeat the enemy, in order to guarantee a happy end.

Once the battle was over, though, and the dead laid out tenderly on the stage, our play ended with a fervent *Hatikvah*, our hymn of hope. That, too, maybe that especially, was part of the myth we were trying to secure. The Arabs of our imagination were a reasonable enemy. True, they did not want to accept Jewish sovereignty in what they considered to be their exclusive domain. True, they would not yield without an armed struggle. Contentious among themselves, they were nevertheless prepared to join forces to push us into the sea. True, true. It would be a terrible war, with many casualties, which is why we Diaspora Jews had to provide Israel with infusions of our blood. But when we won the war, at whatever ghastly price, peace would follow like a curtain being drawn. We were illumined by hope because we thought we could, in the end, determine the outcome of the battle.

One would have thought that after the scale of Hitler's annihilation the Jews would lack the energy for military confrontation. Yet just the opposite was true. Remember your client—was his name Grodzinski?—who had fought in the battle for the road to Jerusalem and went back all the time to visit the graves of fellow soldiers he had barely known? When you told me about him I found it hard to understand why this ill-tempered survivor of Buchenwald should have made his way to Palestine to risk the life he had gone to such lengths to preserve. On the basis of his own testimony he was not a self-sacrificing man and to move from one sphere of death to another seemed out of character. But in the apparent similarity between the corpses of Buchenwald and the dead of Latrun lay the instructive contrast.

At Buchenwald the Jew was erased. A man raised to believe that he had been made in the image of God found that he wasn't even worth comparing to a dog. To be worth nothing, so that no work you could do, no service you could render, would hold as much value for the Germans as reducing you to dust—that was the Jew's experience at Buchenwald. The Germans meant to make it our destiny. Compared with that, war against the Arabs and the British was like returning to human form. Degrading as it may be next to other styles of human association, armed conflict is still a struggle between men and men. Your client was not moving from one field of death to another, but from death to dignity. The proof lies precisely in the graves of his fellow Jewish soldiers that he kept visiting. They *had* graves. He knew even graves must be earned.

Our dignity might have been greater had the Arabs been able to accept our political reality as the British finally did when they withdrew from Palestine in 1948. But the British were exhausted. Having entered World War II with nothing to gain but what they stood to lose, they had drawn on all their resources, in the most important war ever fought, to produce arguably the "finest hour" for this millennium. They had no more stomach for battle in distant lands.

The Arabs were in quite a different mood. Where Europe had drained itself on the fields of slaughter, the Arabs emerged from the war free of their colonial occupiers; poised to consolidate their individual states and a united Arab nation. What an irritant the emerging Jewish state must have presented—irritant, but also opportunity. "The whole Arab people is unalterably opposed to the attempt to impose Jewish immigration and settlement upon it and ultimately to estab- lish a Jewish state in Palestine." Who but we could so have united the otherwise divided Arabs to pronounce the confi- dent phrase, "the whole Arab people"? We were all they had in common. The weakness of the Jews had been amply demonstrated by the Germans, our standing in the commu- nity of nations even more conclusively. With the prospect of Arab hegemony in the Middle East so tantalizingly near, why indeed should they have agreed to share even a speck of land with a people whom civilized Europe had so recently starved, burned, gassed, shot, buried alive, reduced to fertilizer?

Given their perspective, the Arabs would have been fools to accept partition without first trying to destroy the Jewish enemy.

So the gesture of accommodation was withheld, and the Jews had to fight for their sovereignty—like most other nations in world history. Israel suffered over 30,000 dead and wounded in its War of Independence. Yet at that point it still seemed that in denying the Jews their right to the land, the Arabs were denying no more and no less than combatants normally refuse to grant one another and were forcing them to defend what combatants normally must defend. We considered ourselves a war's length from peace.

That optimism lasted over two decades. People who set for Israel between the time my brother's group sailed in 1949 and the summer you and I met in the Sinai in 1969 were "winners" because Israel itself appeared to be on the verge of winning its place in the world. As long as we thought the Arabs would abide by the logic of war we felt ourselves masters of our fate. We Jews had only to prove our determination to remain a sovereign people in our homeland for the Arabs eventually to admit us as worthy enemies, then grudgingly accept us as neighbors, and finally recognize our usefulness as friends.

The Six-Day War felt like final victory. On June 12, 1967, Jews were certain that now, at last, Jordan would sue for some of its lost land, Egypt for the Sinai, even sullen Syria for a strip of the Golan Heights. Israel had just fought the perfect war. It was at this juncture that internal Jewish resistance to Zionism also briefly dissolved. The anti-Israel American Council for Judaism disbanded, and we had reason to believe that it would never reorganize. Even residual Trotskyites paid the country their first tentative visit and found themselves admiring the forests planted by the Jewish National Fund. You could not go much further to impress the skeptics.

I'm not likely to forget the euphoria of the late 1960s, as you and I had our momentary share in it. Instead of the graveyards that had been readied outside Tel Aviv for an estimated 40,000 casualties there were "only" 777 deaths, and a reunited Jerusalem. The Israel Institute for Applied Social Research published its polls on returning the captured territories in exchange for peace, and the figures showed overwhelming majorities of Israelis in a mood of utter magnanimity. After a victory of such scope, Israel had every reason to believe that it could relax its vigilance.

We misjudged the Arabs. They were not the reasonable enemy of our expectations, and their rejection was not subject even to the judgment of war, that final arbiter of political disputes. Quite the opposite. The great victory, which pushed the natural boundaries of Israel to their maximal limits, alerted the Arabs to the outer limit of the Israeli threat. Having lost the most lopsided of modern military confrontations, they discovered they still had the power to deny the victor regional acceptance. We had given them this power. Arab propagandists might trumpet their fear of Jewish expansionism, and circulate the Protocols of the Elders of Zion with its warning of Jewish world conquest, but as surely as Hitler knew, despite his words, that the Jews were not about to take over Europe, so the Arabs knew that the Jews had no ambition to take over the Middle East. Israel wanted a place on the map, and in the Six-Day War it had played its final card. Would the Israelis now march on Damascus? Were they about to seize Amman from King Hussein? Did they covet the beaches of Beirut? Would the Jews return as conquerers to the pyramids? What a joke! The Arabs, an imperial people contemptuous of weakness, saw the Jewish hunger for peace glinting through the Israeli armor, and they knew that they had it in their power to starve us.

I'm now right on the heels of Mrs. Richman's "nowadays," because this is exactly where it began—with the decision on the part of the Arabs to continue their siege and with the dawning realization on the part of the Jews that one more war might not in fact be the last. There seemed to be no way to win the acceptance we had so long pursued. The Jewish people, after suffering six million deaths, might finally have consolidated a country of their own because they could no longer trust in the decency of nations, but the Arabs were about to teach us a deeper lesson: a sovereign Jewish people could be rejected as forcefully as a homeless tribe. The legitimacy of the Jewish state could be denied as ruthlessly as, once, the legitimacy of the Jewish religion.

I don't think we have properly appreciated the genius of the Arab campaign since 1967. (The Jew's tendency to underestimate his enemies has not been tempered even by his experience in this century.) The War of Attrition along the Suez Canal and the Yom Kippur attack of 1973 were in some ways the least of it. More impressive was the growing Arab support for the Palestine Liberation Organization, a radical gang that after 1967 was nursed by the Arab states into a full-scale terrorist army. Arab governments might not be able to transfer their sights from Israeli soldiers to Jewish women and children—at least not without incurring international displeasure and provoking Israel's counterattack—but with safe passports and comfortable bank accounts, "homeless" killers could massacre at will. Israel scored no points with Western European opinion for the agricultural and engineering teams it sent out to underdeveloped countries. These were written off as so much self-promotion. It was the Arab death squads that won European respect. How desperately must Palestinian Arabs desire this land from the Jews if they went to such chilling lengths to eliminate the usurpers! The more Jews the PLO killed, the more it gained the respect of democratic Europe as the legitimate representative of the Palestinian Arabs. As for the Communist rulers of Eastern Europe, they forged the neatest continuity between the first half of the century and the second by locating the PLO terrorist training bases in the same places where the Nazis had trained for the very same activities.

The master stroke of Arab strategy was the war on Zionism. War is said to be the extension of politics, but the Arabs made politics the extension of war. They enlarged their war on Israel into an attack on the idea of Israel. Zionism, the Jewish claim to a land of their own, was declared racist because it deprived Palestinian Arabs of *their* homeland. If you believe in the force of ideas you have to grant the Arabs their triumph, because they destroyed at a stroke what it had taken us over a century to achieve.

The keys to Arab political success were the substitution of "homeless Palestinian" for homeless Jew and the inversion of all the facts and terms of the Jewish national struggle. The same "whole Arab people" that had been "unalterably opposed to . . . a Jewish state in Palestine" now accused the Jews of having denied that state to the Palestinian Arabs. The Arabs, having themselves first rendered the Palestinians homeless by refusing to accept partition in 1948 and having kept them homeless by refusing to resettle in their vast lands those who needed a home, now blamed this condition of homelessness on the Jews. And, indeed, they had their evidence. After more than four decades, incredibly, the camps are still there, while of the million Jewish refugees from Arab lands, Israel today shows hardly a living trace. As soon as they could, Israelis replaced the tin-roofed transit shacks where the refugees broiled in summer and froze in winter by modern apartments, that may not satisfy our aesthetic taste or the full needs of their residents, but are hardly designed to elicit from the outside world sympathy for banished Jews. In the meantime, the country has absorbed hundreds of thousands of additional refugees from what used to be the Soviet Union, Ethiopia, South America. The Arab states, for their part, cultivated refugees the way some raise orchids, with the result that they now boast generations of destitute women and children. Everywhere the homeless Palestinians appear with their stigmata to charge the Zionists with usurpation, racism, genocide.

It's funny, isn't it, that the Arabs, who place such value on military prowess, should have lost on the battlefield, while the Jews, who take pride in the power of their intellect, should have lost the war of ideas? By declaring the illegitimacy of Zionism the Arabs not only robbed us of our rightful claims on them but charged us with the very crime of which they rightly stood accused. Within less than a decade they deprived us of our moral advantage and reestablished us as a suspect nation that threatens the human equilibrium.

You know better than I how this works. You're the one who explained to me that there is no crime before the law if no one is prepared to lay a charge. Thus, Jordan does not allow a Jew to reside within its borders and discriminates even against Jewish tourists. Jordanian law condemns an Arab to death for selling land to a Jew! Yet Jordan will never be indicted for racism, because there is no Jew self-respecting enough to press the charge. The Arabs have in any case preempted any moral or legal claims that we may have brought against them by accusing us of the original sin of entry into the Middle East to drain the swamps, plant the vineyards, and build Tel Aviv. As my mother says, *Az men fregt a shayle vert tref:* you have only to put the question for the rabbi to pronounce the thing unclean. At the same Table of Nations that once credited our right to exist, our legitimacy is called daily into question. We stand accused—as by Christians through the centuries for the murder of Jesus—not for what is correctible, but for the fact of our national existence. No physical harm the Arabs can ever do us is as great as this accusation, because the charge justifies all the harm they will ever do us, calls it forth as a holy mission.

Mona Richman, apparently oblivious to Arab propaganda, nevertheless responds to the continuing barrage through her disappointment in a declining Israel. The real source of her anxiety is too dangerous to confront. When the Arabs revived in bold new form the accusation of our illegitimacy, they themselves may not have realized the potency of their idea among those whom the Mona Richmans of the world feel they must answer to. I mean, of course, the court of liberal opinion which has never felt wholly comfortable with the Jews as a people. Beginning with that great enlightener Voltaire, many of the leading continental rationalists, liberals, and radicals expressed their suspicion of Jewry, as if it were perfectly acceptible for other peoples to transfer their waning religious identity to forms of national identification, treacherous only in the case of the Jews. Without the destruction of European Jewry who knows whether the modern state of Israel could have won enough liberal support to gain any Western recognition at all? Yet the Jewish state was born, muting at least some of the hostility to Jewish national revival. Now came the Arabs to stoke its smoldering ashes back into a fiery blaze. Let's face it: knowing on our flesh the consequence of anti-Jewish ideas, we have good reason to lie awake at night over the knowledge that the Arabs consider the Jews expendable and want to persuade the rest of the world that Israel should be destroyed. Mona Richman, who values her sleep, finds it more convenient to attribute to the Jewish state the failure of her hopes for it.

I hope you don't get the impression from the turn of my letter that it is meant to protect you. It's not Israel's reputation that's in question but our deceit. In today's issue of the *Canadian Jewish News* (one of the many pleasures you've sacrificed in moving away from here) a luncheon speaker is quoted as describing the disenchantment of Diaspora Jews with Israel as "the cooling passion of a normal marriage." In 1948, he says, we saw Israel through the adoring eyes of newlyweds. Now, after over forty years of marriage, we find it hard to credit the wife of youth with even a single charm. The audience, which must have overlooked the falsehood as well as the vulgarity of sentiment, is said to have applauded.

If long-married couples are supposedly so bored with each other, why do Israelis these days look so lovingly on us? Hardly the irksome mate in an arid union, we Diaspora Jews seem to have released in our spouses a warmer, deeper affection. Israel's intellectuals, politicians, and businessmen flirt with us as never before. And indeed, why shouldn't they appreciate our value? Thriving in America on a continent of apparently limitless resources, we are spared the affront of hostility. Our sons are taken in marriage by the untitled princesses of the land. Our manifold flaws are no longer of much interest even to satirists. No one abhors us—only they, the occupiers of Zion, now give us a bad name. In a grotesque reversal, it is the Israelis who are now charged with poisoning the wells, while the majority of Jews in the lands of plenty live a life of normalcy such as the Jewish people has always dreamed of. With ultimate irony, we are attacked only for aiding *you*, for declaring ourselves Zionists. Thus, not only are we diaspora Jews in democratic countries relieved of the physical need to protect the Jewish state, we incur the displeasure of our countrymen only when we bother ourselves to help in your defense.

Our Israeli bride was once irresistible to us because she brought us the dowry of international good will. Now that the Arabs and their various sponsors and toadies have smeared her with the filth of their loathing, she has begun to assume for us too the twisted shape of the ghetto Jew. Why look, we say, she is full of warts: her democracy is endan-

Prologue: Letter to a New Israeli

gered, her greed corrupts the purity of her soul, her fanatics are flourishing, her economy is faltering, her leaders flounder. Our disappointment, whose source is in the Arabs and in ourselves—in them for so irrationally rejecting our presence, in ourselves for not conclusively affirming it—we attribute ever more self-righteously, belligerently, to the Jewish state.

Am I absurd, barely forty-eight hours after your departure, to begin addressing you as an Israeli, with a sense of much more than geographic distance between us? Now that you have your identity card, are you suddenly the magnified Other? I'm reminded of my first years as a teacher, when I was assigned to teach a survey of English literature to engineering students. Considerately I prepared my lectures on Chaucer and Spenser with analogies to slide rules, bridge construction, and electrical sockets—until a delegation of young men came to say that they had really a normal range of interests and would appreciate my lectures more if I just treated them the way I would anyone else. I will not forget the lesson they taught me in the dangers of artificial differentiation, and I'm even less likely to forget how much you and I have in common. But the differences I note are true, as I can show by a simple example.

Tomorrow night, when it comes, first for you and seven hours later for me, we will both be sitting with our families watching the evening news. Coincidentally, both your family and mine will be tuned in to our neighbor's broadcast; we because we prefer the range of U.S. coverage; you for the linguistic convenience of Jordan's prime-time news in English. My children will feel beside them the protective shield of the freest country in the world, and let us hope the strongest. To be sure, one or another of their trendy teachers will have warned them of the dangers of cultural oppression, and tried to sell them on the charms of victim-chic, but they are smart enough to know themselves blessed.

Your children, meanwhile, will feel themselves brushed by the political intentions of a mean state that projects its weather map of the region without any sign of Israel on it—neither small, medium, nor large. One night in the Jewish homeland, and they will know themselves despised, rejected, contingent. No doubt one of their teachers will pretend that such details don't matter, given the essential brotherhood of the human race. The children are smart enough to know themselves threatened.

You will do a good job assuring your family that their country is sufficiently powerful to withstand its enemies, and so, for the moment, it may be. But what can shield them from the hate? Will you try to teach them that God's protecting love must compensate for the destructive will of the Arabs? Will you try to teach them that adversity strengthens? Will you remind them that as Sadat came at last to Jerusalem, so too will the other Arab rulers, each in his time, and, one hopes, in theirs? Jewish hope has been a questionable asset in this century, and if you are going to feed it to your children, they'd be well advised to live on tight rations. Tell them Sadat's coming makes their odds on the Arabs a little better, at least, than the odds on our vaunted messiah.

We learn from Hillel in *The Wisdom of the Fathers:* "If I am not for myself, who will be for me? And being for myself, what am I? And if not now, when?" According to the

Prologue: Letter to a New Israeli

Talmudic rabbis and rabbinic commentators, this compressed dialectic had to do with the individual accumulation of merit through adhering to the prescribed Jewish way of life; a person should acquire merit for himself and not depend on others to perform good deeds on his behalf; and since he is under equal obligation to make others do good, he should also teach others the right way. But the Jewish folk came to understand Hillel's teaching corporately, as a political directive that they should not expect anyone else to stand up on their behalf unless they have first learned to stand up for themselves. Primo Levi, who survived almost a full year in Auschwitz, entitled his novel about a band of Jewish partisans *If Not Now, When?*, citing these words from a partisan song:

> *Brothers, away from this Europe of graves:*
> *Let us climb together towards the land*
> *Where we will be men among men.*
> *If I'm not for myself, who will be for me?*
> *If not this way, how? If not now, when?*

For the partisans, and for us, the words of Hillel became a Zionist imperative. Because the Jewish struggle for freedom is always launched against political despotism, it benefits everyone else who truly clings to freedom. But it follows from this imperative that if we Jews fail to stand up for ourselves we also fail the cause of freedom.

Of course, the Jewish idea of fraternal obligation is only an acute instance of mutual responsibility on an international scale. Our political situation is not unique, except to the degree that Jews have become the target for the most active aggressors, requiring of us a special vigilance. We are obliged to figure out what benefits our enemies gain from this pursuit of us, what pressure their enmity brings to bear on us. Since anti-Semitism could never succeed without the collusion of liberal democracies, we have to understand how presumably well-intentioned people choose to betray the Jews, and how presumably well-intentioned Jews come to favor the cause of their antagonists over their own.

Now that you're gone, I'll try to think through some of the things we used to talk about. I'll leave the personal problems between us for the time being to concentrate on the political predicament we share. I may not be able to share your tax burden or your soldiering, nor any of the greater delights of residence in a Jewish country, but I can try to see what you're up against. What follows is my version of a love letter.

Chapter One

Liberalism For and Against the Jews

Jews are associated with liberalism the way the French are with wine: it is considered native to their region. Every once in a while a French politician, whether because of an ulcer or the political debt he owes to dairy farmers, will astonish the world by promoting the benefits of milk, but these deviations do not affect the overall association in the slightest. So, too, the association of the Jews with liberalism appears to grow stronger the more it is opened to challenge. As I use it, liberalism is a belief in rationality and a rational approach to political questions; in freedom for the individual within a constitutional, participatory democracy; in cultural pluralism within an open society; and in the rule of law. Liberals believe in progress and in the progressive improvement of human society. (The debate within liberalism between

21

extreme egalitarians and anarchists has only a peripheral bearing on our subject.) Underlying all these liberal positions is an attitude of hopefulness regarding human nature. As tolerant folk who want only to live and let live, liberals trust that all human problems are amenable to negotiated solutions, that all people are united in a spirit of brotherhood, and that history itself is a record of progress. They detest the use of force, not only for the damage it causes but because in admitting the limits of reason it throws humankind back to a more primitive stage of civilization. The pure liberal spirit precludes the possibility of intractable hatred or intransigent political will.

As this broad definition suggests, the attachment of modern Jews to liberalism seems virtually axiomatic, since it was the precondition for their emancipation. When autocratic monarchies began to give way to constitutional participatory government, it was the spirit of liberalism that championed rights of citizenship. Those who fought on behalf of the Jews did not necessarily do so out of love or understanding, but because the Jews were the most prominent targets of discrimination in a still less-than-perfect society.

"Let us concede that the Jews may be more morally corrupt than other nations; that they are guilty of a proportionately greater number of crimes than the Christians, that their character in general inclines more toward usury and fraud in commerce, that their religious prejudice is more antisocial and clannish; but I must add that this supposed greater moral corruption of the Jews is a necessary and natural consequence of the oppressed condition in which they have been living for so many centuries." So wrote Christian Wilhelm von Dohm,

Liberalism For and Against the Jews

exemplar of the German Enlightenment and friend of Moses Mendelssohn, in his 1781 essay "On the Civil Improvement of the Jews," an argument for amelioration of the civil status of the Jews that influenced King Joseph II's pathbreaking Edict of Tolerance.

Dohm's ideas of the Jews were still smeared by inherited prejudice, as Mendelssohn pointed out in a passionate rejoinder. But being predicated on reason in the first place, they were open to the same evolutionary clarification that he foresaw in the civil condition of the Jews. Dohm believed that happiness was the legitimate goal of all human beings, and that it could be achieved universally if good government were to "weaken the influence of religious principles and abolish the mutual antipathy which is only nurtured by persecution."

Many European Jews placed their hopes in these ideas of progress. They naturally hoped that this enlightened view of human nature would finally give them a chance to prove their merit and to disprove the misconceptions that held sway in the minds of their fellow citizens. In seeking acceptance, such Jews could only hope to find allies among the liberals who believed in tolerance and individual rights, since the conservatives who opposed these views upheld a way of life that had made a virtue out of persecuting them.

Moreover, some of the energy of liberalism seemed to emerge straight out of Jewish teachings. Freedom is a cardinal virtue of the Jewish way of life, reconfirmed every year in the reenactment of the Exodus at Passover and in the celebration of Succoth, when Jews live in roofless huts as a reminder of the existential conditions of desert travel. Jewish tradition kept alive the meaning of liberty by connecting the Exodus story with the imperative of kindness to strangers. The moral impulse of liberalism also seemed derived from the Hebrew prophets. They had demanded individual accountability of their monarchs, awakened compassion for the downtrodden, and with what seemed to be defiance of the priests and of tradition, had championed the spirit of the law over its mechanical observance.

Even reason, assumed by some Christian proponents of enlightenment to be the antonym of religion, was fundamental to the Jewish religious tradition, which gave the rabbis full authority to determine what was permissible on the basis of their interpretation of the law. The Jewish belief in a potential messiah rather than one who had already come further reinforced the distinction between the natural and supernatural spheres, while the absence of any fixed religious authority and the Jewish goal of universal literacy encouraged the development of a relatively democratic community of thinkers. All in all, when German-Jewish religious reformers and East-European Jewish secular thinkers embraced the ideas of liberalism in the eighteenth and nineteenth centuries, they could feel the new positions arising naturally out of their own language and experience.

If liberalism, then, is the necessary precondition for the advancement of Jews in modern society, and if it is at the same time perceived by Jews as the outgrowth of their own indigenous civilization, one can hardly wonder at the tight association of modern Jews with liberal ideas. Indeed, the Jews would appear to be the very touchstone of liberalism. A society's acceptance of them establishes that it is becoming more tolerant as a result of intelligent human effort, that the rule of law holds firm, that individual rights are respected, and that human nature is open to rational persuasion.

But here the problem arises. For suppose that liberalism cannot protect the Jews? Instead of the improvement of European society that liberals anticipated, suppose there had occurred a severe deterioration in the condition of the Jews, culminating in their mass destruction, and that this deterioration had occurred among the very people who had promoted all the ideas of rational progress? What would this destruction of the Jews do to the faith in liberalism and to the axiomatic association of liberalism with the Jews?

Were human history a scientific experiment, the answer to this question would be obvious. If liberalism guarantees equal rights to the Jews and if Jews are the chief representatives and beneficiaries of liberalism in the modern age, then a failure to protect the Jews signifies either that the hypothesis of liberalism is faulty or that the experiment has been improperly conducted. In other words, if the Jews of Europe were destroyed rather than advanced, either liberalism was mistaken in its trust in rationality and human progress, or else it did not control those values carefully and rigorously enough. Confronted with failure on such a massive scale, with the inversion rather than the proof of its hypothesis, science would certainly reexamine its fundamental premises. But despite its belief in reason, liberalism is not scientific. It is a species of faith, and it has responded to the failure of its premises in the way that true believers routinely do, by ignoring and glossing over the contrary evidence. Before the Holocaust, liberals routinely blamed the Jews for the inability of liberalism to protect them. Nineteenth-century supporters of the Enlightenment told the Jews that they were being oppressed because they had not yet learned the language of the land or proven their civility through the adoption of western costume. German reformers said that Judaism would become acceptable to Christians if it adapted some of its ritual to local norms and eliminated its national character. Social reformers of various hues told the Jews that if they ceased to be royal financiers and bankers, economic parasites, or unproductive middlemen, and became farmers or proletarians, they would be appreciated by their fellow citizens and comrades. In the absence of deeply held religious faith, liberalism became synonymous for its adherents with an optimistic outlook on life, and many of those adherents— including many Jews—would sooner have sacrificed their lives than their optimism. The choice was even simpler when the lives to be sacrificed were not their own.

The problem has only hardened since the destruction of the European Jews. There are still many people who want to believe that all human problems are amenable to reasoned solutions, that all people are united in the spirit of brotherhood, that history is a record of progress. The true believers among them preclude the possibility of hatred and premeditated aggression. At the same time, there undeniably are still rulers and politicians who want to destroy the Jews; they think the Jews take up too much room and now occupy space that belongs rightfully to them. Indeed, the European precedent persuades many Arabs that conquest of Israel is only a matter of time. That the fate of the Jews is inextricably bound up with liberalism no one can deny. But in the present as in the past, when actual Jew-hatred challenges the

Liberalism For and Against the Jews

principles of liberal faith, the inconvenient Jewish variable is always in danger of being sacrificed to the purity of liberal ideals.

The sociologist Nathan Glazer is one of the most prominent interpreters of Jewish liberalism in America. Professor of Education and Social Structure at Harvard University and co-editor with Irving Kristol of the periodical *The Public Interest*, Glazer has written authoritatively on many aspects of American Jewish life, including American Jewish religion and the effect on Jews of what he calls "affirmative discrimination." His 1991 summary of "Jews and American Liberalism" offers the following interpretation of Jewish voting patterns and political trends:

> A recent major study of religion in America tells us what we all know: that Jews are the most liberal religious group in America. They have the smallest number of persons declaring themselves Republicans, the largest number declaring themselves to be Democrats. More detailed analysis of this survey would undoubtedly also reveal the great anomaly of Jewish liberalism, one which has been evident in studies for 40 years: political allegiance in the United States is affected most strongly by economic status, but Jews break the pattern. The most prosperous of all religious groups, they are also the most liberal . . . by any measure one can think of.

Glazer also quotes the famous observation of Milton Himmelfarb, the dean of American Jewish sociologists, that the Jews earn like Episcopalians but vote like Puerto Ricans, and he cites as evidence the fact that when New York elected its first black mayor, David Dinkins, the only whites who gave him a substantial part of their vote were Jews.

On the facts of the case there appears to be universal agreement. All the pollsters on this continent concur that "American Jews stand firmly to the Left," defying the political drift toward conservatism in America at large. A survey by the *Los Angeles Times* in 1989 reported that half the Jews polled locally cited "a commitment to social equality" as the chief characteristic of their Jewish identity as against only 17 percent who chose religious observance and about the same number who cited support for Israel. As in the Reform Movement that swept Germany in the nineteenth century, and in the popular Jewish secular movements of Eastern Europe at the beginning of this century, there are Jews today for whom liberalism is more than a political preference. It is the strongest expression of their Jewish identity.

Not only do Jews continue to express their commitment to social equality, open immigration policy, and left-wing causes far beyond their proportion in the American population and contrary to the sociological pattern of their economic group, but they have lately begun to return to these positions *as Jews.* Thus a typical new charity, the Jewish World Service, was founded on the East coast in the mid-1980s by some well-to-do Jews who, recognizing "the imperative within the Jewish moral and ethical tradition to assist both Jews and non-Jews," determined to extend their assistance to the suffering victims of the Third World. The Jewish Fund for Justice was founded in 1984 "to provide a Jewish presence in efforts to alleviate poverty in the United States" and "to assist low-income groups undertaking grass-roots organizing efforts around the country." The organization Mazon: A Jewish Response to Hunger was founded in 1985 by Leonard Fein, then-editor of *Moment* magazine. It asks Jews to contribute a small percentage of the money they spend on such celebrations as weddings and bar mitzvahs "to help the hungry and homeless in the United States and abroad." While the founders of these admirable charities invariably locate their impulse in Jewish ethical tradition, they do not explain why Jewish charity to non-Jews could not have continued, as in the past, through the many hundreds of non-denominational charities in which Jews have been prominent and to which they have always contributed generously. Nor do they explain why these Jewish charities-for-others should have arisen in America at the same time.

The same sectarian impulse also characterizes the left-wing magazine *Tikkun*, which was founded in Berkeley in 1986 with the modest wish "to heal, repair, and transform the world." Jewish intellectuals in the immediate post-war period took for granted their right to speak for all Americans in a non-denominational framework and contributed to publications like *Commentary* and *Dissent* that spoke directly to the centers of political and intellectual power. *Tikkun*, however —as its title suggests—marked a return to the model of English and Yiddish socialist publications of the 1930's by addressing a specifically Jewish audience and by interpreting world events mainly in terms of their Jewish significance. The magazine's founding editorial statement affirmed a belief that the "liberal and progressive forces, non-Jewish and Jewish alike, including the Democratic party, the labor movement, the women's movement, the anti-nuclear and peace movement, the movements for equality and economic justice—all have something important to learn from Judaism and the experience of the Jewish people," since (according to this editor) the Jewish religion "is irrevocably committed to the side of the oppressed." The translation of religious into political categories is here taken for granted as the basis of a new kind of Jewish liberation theology.

The explanation for this sociopolitical anomaly—the return of a *Jewish* left or of *Jewish* liberalism at a time when no such corresponding trend is apparent among other ethnic groups—is generally sought in the Jewish religion or in Jewish suffering. Liberal spokesman Peter Steinfels recently wrote approvingly in the *New York Times* that "religious tradition and historical experience converge in the Jewish inclination to challenge the status quo." Citing the strong attraction of liberal and socialist movements for the oppressed European Jews of the nineteenth century, he assumes that Jews remain loyal, and ought to remain loyal, to those earlier causes.

Glazer more soberly shows that the association of American Jews with liberalism was originally rooted at least partly in self-interest. Workers and small businessmen favored progressive taxation and some measure of redistribution that would benefit them; new immigrants felt at home in the Democratic Party, which was traditionally the party of immigrants; as members of a persecuted minority, Jews fought discrimination on grounds of race, color, and religion because they required a more tolerant society. But then, turning from the 1930s to the present, Glazer unaccountably concludes as follows:

Liberalism For and Against the Jews

Self interest, I would argue, no longer explains Jewish adherence to liberalism. The Jewish businessman and professional, if he were following his self-interest, would by now have become a Republican, as his Catholic and Protestant business and professional colleagues have become. The Jewish suburbanite, if he were following his self-interest, would have joined his Catholic neighbors in moving from the Democratic to the Republican Party. Despite the presence of a substantial number of Jewish neo-conservative —and conservative—intellectuals who argue that the United States is not helped by the economic policies of liberalism, and business is certainly not helped by it, they find few followers among American Jews. Jewish self-interest is no longer served by the civil-rights agenda, as it has moved from color-blindness to color preference. But that too does not trouble Jews too much. Their traditional commitment to liberalism is such that they are willing to go along with it.

Glazer is here telling us that the "tradition" of liberalism is so powerful among American Jews that they adhere to it despite the fact that it no longer represents their political interests, and although many of them are traditional in no other sense. To my knowledge, no other sociologist has offered any stronger explanation than this for the atypical political behavior of Jews, accepting the premise that Jews are atypical because they are Jews.

A second leading American Jewish intellectual, Irving Kristol, is impatient with Jews for doing what Glazer says they do—that is, remaining liberals against what he believes to be their self-interest. Kristol, who along with Norman Podhoretz is the most powerful and articulate voice of neo-conservatism in America, traces the left-of-center position of American Jews on the political spectrum to "the combination of secular historical experience and the religious mutation it provoked." He identifies as some of the formative causes of this orientation the radical strains of liberalism that influenced their European Jewish forebears; the oppression and anti-Semitism that made them welcome its egalitarian promise; the prophetic teachings within the tradition that provided an ideological vocabulary and impetus for secular messianism; and American social conditions facing the Jewish immigrants that promoted identification with the Democratic Party in particular. In contrast to Steinfels and the editors of *Tikkun*, Kristol does not approve of the aberrant Jewish identification of the Jews with liberalism. But since he is no more able than they to account for it, he predicts that this situation cannot last. The increasing irrelevance of socialism as an economic or political model, and the "cognitive dissonance" fostered in American Jews by the gap between their inherited political ideas and their situation—particularly their concern for the State of Israel—will gradually wean many of them from the left. Thus because Kristol agrees that Jewish liberalism is not politically self-serving—but because he also believes that the Jews are no less rational than others—he is certain that the Jews will eventually give it up.

In this belief he is no less mistaken than Steinfels and Glazer. American Jews will probably continue to identify with liberalism in even greater numbers not because they are irrational—but precisely because they think they *are* acting in their political self-interest.

Liberalism For and Against the Jews

The so-called aberrant theory of Jewish liberalism omits
the single most important determining factor of Jewish
political experience, namely the effectiveness and virulence
at any given moment of anti-Jewish politics; not "racism,"
"discrimination," or any other such general intolerance but
the political attempt to stigmatize the Jews as the cause of
regional or international malaise. To overlook anti-Semitism
in assessing the political behavior of Jews is like overlooking
race in assessing the behavior of black Americans; yet social
scientists do it as a matter of course, perhaps even as a matter
of faith. In fact, Jews vote exceptionally in relation to other
ethnic and religious minorities because of their present
historical role, not because of their political history, nor any
putative innate or inherited moral strengths (a strange claim,
certainly, for people who abjure theories of religio-racial
supremacy). Rather it is due to the unique political pressures
to which they are subject. What appears to be the odd
pattern of well-educated, relatively wealthy, and rapidly
assimilating Jews voting against their economic and social
interests is in reality the pattern of acculturated Jews trying to
escape the political trap they feel closing around them.

Although I intend to examine Arab propaganda in the
following chapter, its effect on liberalism requires some
mention here. The Arab charge that the creation of Israel is a
crime against an Arab people has much in common with the
earlier Christian charge that Jews denied the Son of God, or
that of the Nazis that Jews polluted the Aryan race. These
charges are unanswerable except through dissolution of the
Jewish religion, the Jewish people, the Jewish state. Jews
cannot respond to such charges because they do not regard

them as crimes; yet because they cannot respond, they have no way of clearing their name. Whereas the Arab wars against Israel between 1948 and 1973 had targeted only the Jews of Israel, the Arab propaganda campaign that began in the mid-1970's attacked the Jews in democratic countries with charges of corrupt association and were aimed increasingly, and with ever greater refinement, at them in particular. The more unpopular the Arabs were able to make Israel, the more Jews outside Israel tried to win back their own popularity by proving their innocence.

The paradoxical political behavior of American Jews could in fact much more accurately be described as the desire to dissociate oneself from a people under attack by advertising one's own goodness. There is no other ethnic, racial, or religious minority in America, apart from the Jews, so many of whose members publicly disclaim responsibility for the "evils" of their own people and land. There is nothing among Roman Catholics analogous to the newly resuscitated American Council for Judaism that is devoted to undoing the Jewish state; no intellectual of another ethnic group who argues, as does Noam Chomsky, for the dissolution of the homeland of his people. There is no lobbying group among Greeks, Blacks, Poles, or protestants analogous to Jerome Segal's Jewish Peace lobby in Washington, which tries to limit rather than extend United States support for Israel. There is no cohort in the media (among black Americans, for example, or Irish Americans, or Arab Americans) comparable to the Jews who specialize in exposing the failings of Israel. While it is certainly true that liberal Americans often hold their own country in relatively low esteem, and have been known to attack its weaknesses in the name of forcing its improvement, America has not been surrounded from the moment of its founding by countries committed to its extinction. Hence it may not appear to require the support of each and every American quite to the same degree. By contrast, Jews are a very tiny people with multitudinous and powerful enemies. Yet Jews are the only American minority whose members do not as a matter of course support the land of their people, and some of whose members join in the political effort against it. The banner under which they manifest this aberrant political activity is liberalism, or the Left.

Consider the case of an American Jew who according to the sociologists is acting unusually by his continuing association with liberalism. Let us say he is a successful businessman, board member of a bank that has dealings with oil companies, Arab investors, and other businessmen affected by the Arab boycott. Before 1975, when Israel was widely perceived as the noble underdog of the Middle East, he did not have to apologize for being a Jew. Once Israel began to be refashioned in the media, however, as a belligerent and intransigent state that foments international unrest because of its unwillingness to "give up land for peace," a state that oppresses poor Palestinian Arabs and brutalizes their women and children—how comfortable can the poor Jew (who is in every other sense a rich Jew) feel encountering these charges day after day? Whenever something touches on Israel and the Arab boycott, on Arab investments and Arab loans, he will find himself implicated as his fellow board members are not. His Jewishness will have become an issue because in prosecuting their war against the Jews the Arabs will have made it one. It sets him apart from all the others around the table, whose ancestral homes and ethnic families are not being charged with crimes against humanity. How will he react to this unfair political isolation?

The confident and firm Jew will take on the battle against Arab propaganda in the boardroom the same way he would defend anything else he believed in but with the added incentive of protecting his own people. He would explain as often and as well as he could the reasons for maintaining just banking policies in the face of undue pressures and for protecting Israel politically against defamation as well as against military incursions. He would have to weigh very carefully his efforts on behalf of the Jews against many other considerations: his duties as an officer, the fiscal policy of the institution he is serving, his ambition, his own business interests, the political inclinations of his colleagues and the degree of their intimacy outside the board, and not least, his own temperament. But were he to act as most other people would do in defense of their threatened group, he would have to become at least a foot soldier in the propaganda war against his people.

Suppose, however, that he is neither a firm nor a confident Jew but one who feels his Jewishness to be a burden or knows very little about it, or who in marrying a non-Jewish wife and moving into higher business and banking circles gradually left his Jewishness behind, like an old skin? Suppose that he doesn't care, one way or another, about Israel at all? Or else, while caring, he wishes that Israel did not make his own life uncomfortable. Such feelings would not be a crime. One of the greatest benefits of the American way of life is in having

Liberalism For and Against the Jews

made voluntary the kinds of identification that were compulsory in Europe. One can only be relieved and grateful that in America, no Jew has to remain Jewish if he doesn't want to.

But the Arab offensive against the Jewish state cramps this freedom and sets Jews unwillingly apart from their fellow Americans. Unlike the military assaults against Israel that left the reputation of American Jews intact, or associated them with innocent victims, the propaganda war against Zionism brushes them with the moral taint of illegitimacy. The relation of an Italian to Italy or an Irishman to Ireland is not called into question; no one challenges Italy's sovereignty, and even in the aftermath of IRA bombings, the British do not call Irish nationalism "racist," or otherwise provoke Irish Americans into vilifying their homeland. Where there is no accusation of collective guilt, there is no need for members of the group to protest their innocence. But in singling out the Jews as the only people not entitled to a land, Arabs accuse Jewish supporters of Israel for the crime of national affiliation.

Many a queasy Jewish board member tries to solve the problem by defining himself as a liberal. Don't look at me, he says to himself and his colleagues. I am one of the nicest fellows that ever lived; I am open-minded, tolerant, adaptable, and forward-looking—all the things associated with liberal optimism; I support all the other minorities, even against my own economic interests. Moreover, I don't even necessarily support the Jewish state, which is said to be causing so much trouble in the Middle East. Yes, I support the good and noble Israel that takes in refugees and gives up conquered territories. But when it comes to the Palestinians, I would no more stand up for Israel than I would for any other wicked oppressor. I am even willing to dissociate myself publicly from Israel, to "dissent" from my fellow Jews in order to prove my fairmindedness, as long as you do not tar me with the brush of your disapproval and set me artificially apart. Liberalism among such board members and leftism among intellectuals are the Jew's attempt to parry or deflect the forces of hatred. As his enemies try to drive a wedge between the Jews and all the others, he tries to demonstrate his attachment to the others by proving his independence from the Jews.

The proliferation of Jewish nondenominational charities such as the Jewish Fund for Justice, and other public avowals of kindliness and liberalism, are similar attempts by Jews to counteract the Arab claim of Jewish immorality. The Jewish will to goodness may be a wonderful thing, but not when it comes at the expense of defending the Jews as a people.

Nathan Glazer, in his remarks on the liberalism of American Jews, sees that Israel is the key to the anomalous condition he describes. But rather than explain how and why Israel burdens the Jews (whereas Italy never burdens the Italians, nor Ireland the Irish), he accounts for the first anomaly by invoking a second.

> If Jews become divided from the liberalism to which they have been attached for two-thirds of this century, it is because of Israel, and the way Israel introduces complex cross-currents in liberal positions, and in Jewish positions. When Israel was founded, these cross-currents were ignored. Israel was a country of refuge for survivors of Nazism, its founding was supported by the victorious powers in World War II, it was a democratic nation in a part of the world

Liberalism For and Against the Jews

where democracy was rare or nonexistent, and a social democratic nation in a part of the world in which the rich and powerful dominated and exploited the poor. Why should not liberals have been supporters of Israel? And they were, pushing aside a fatal flaw, the dispossession of the Arabs of Palestine, a flaw which has grown to giant proportions, making almost impossible the effort to bridge the growing gap between the support of Israel and liberal positions on a host of issues.

This analysis raises many more questions than it answers. What "complex cross-currents" could Israel have introduced in liberal positions that were not similarly introduced by more than a hundred other new nations? Since Arab opposition to the growing Jewish presence in Palestine gained momentum through the 1920s and 1930s, and seven Arab armies attacked Israel at the moment of its founding, how could liberals once have overlooked the "dispossession of the Arabs"? And why, having once been invisible, should this flaw suddenly have grown, as weirdly as Alice on mushrooms, to giant proportions?

Had Glazer mentioned the unmentionable in his analysis there would have been no mystery at all. Liberalism became a "tradition" among American Jews because they were seeking in its promise of tolerance and brotherhood an end to their exceptional fate at the hands of anti-Semites. The Jews valued liberalism more than their money, because without acceptance, money profited them little more than Shylock's. In liberalism, they sought individual refuge from the hatred that pursued them collectively as Jews. Thus Israel was popular among liberals for twenty-five years when it appeared to put an end to anti-Semitism. Its liberal popularity began to decline the minute the Arabs resuscitated ideological anti-Semitism in the 1970s, made it the axis of an Arab-Communist alliance, and notified the world that they felt thoroughly *justified* in destroying Israel, and indeed expected help from the international community in achieving their ends.

Anti-Semitism discomfits liberals by forcing them to abandon their pacific, generous, optimistic view of the world in order to take account of a specific, aggressive, and declared intention of destroying—yet again—the Jews. It forces Jews, in particular, into the humiliating position of having to modify their own ambitions in order to thwart the ambitions of their enemies. Many American Jews, preferring a life of their own choosing to a life dictated by Arab rejectionism, refuse to acknowledge the assault against their people whom they would otherwise be expected to assist. Having once embraced Israel as the solution to anti-Semitism, they now join in attacking it as the provocation of anti-Semitism, the only thing that can threaten their peace of mind. They rededicate themselves to liberalism, in the hope that its view of political nature will actually prevail, and in order to camouflage what would otherwise appear a cowardly defection from their people, for the second time in this century.

In Glazer's entire historical overview of "Jews and American Liberalism," there is no single reference to the Arab war against the Jewish state, nor the war of ideas that the Arabs launched in the early 1970's to prove that the creation of Israel "dispossessed the Arabs of Palestine." The omission in this study of the key variable in effecting the change it describes allows the author to treat liberalism independently of the Arab war against the Jews—a double omission, since that war has liberalism as its target as well as the Jewish state. Not Israel, but the war against it, introduced "complex cross-currents" in liberal positions; just as the war against the Jews had complicated liberalism before Israel was created. The complexity derived in each case from the illiberal war against the Jews, not from their own unexceptional will to live.

If Glazer's analysis fails as sociology, it nevertheless serves as a perfect specimen of American Jewish liberalism. In particular, the phrase "a fatal flaw" gives warning of things to come. What is one to make of these words in an objective sociological analysis? Sociologists have shown that when white people refer to black skin as flawed, they are judging by the standard of their own color, then using that evidence to legitimate the enslavement of black people who are doomed to their fate. Similarly, it is the Arabs who determine that Israel is "a flaw," just as they considered the Jews religiously flawed when they did not become Muslim. This flaw is in the eye of the beholder. The existence of Israel is assuredly not a flaw in the eyes of Jews whose tradition of many millennia has led them to reclaim it politically, nor in the eyes of international law, which acknowledged the legitimacy of many dozens of new states (including twenty-two Arab states) in this century alone.

The flaw is fatal because the Arabs have made themselves the instruments of Israel's negative fate. As Glazer intuits, Israel has also become "fatal" for liberals, for it denies their belief in a world of brotherhood, rationality, and negotiable solutions. The defense of Israel against the Arabs, as against earlier anti-Semites, would require of liberals the kind of sustained exertion in the realm of ideas and political action that Israelis have had to manifest in the military defense of their country. Instead, many liberals sacrifice the Jews to liberal pieties and find that Israel is no longer a worthy cause.

Nathan Glazer's altogether typical account of changing American Jewish attitudes toward Israel—a description that omits any reference to the Arab war of ideas—proves that the Arabs have enjoyed unqualified success in blaming Israel for their endless war against it. In their comparison of Israeli and American Jews, *Two Worlds of Judaism*, Charles S. Liebman and Steven M. Cohen similarly omit any mention of Arab propaganda, finding much to praise in the "fidelity to Jewish tradition" of American Jews and something to apologize for in the behavior of Israelis. We know why Arab governments mounted a campaign of defamation against Israel: because they wanted to justify in the language of morality the crime they intend to commit, sooner or later, through force of arms. The more interesting question is how and why anti-Semitism continues to achieve its goals in a world that is thought to be governed by "victorious" liberal principles.

Chapter Two

The Twentieth Century's Most Durable Ideology

Contrary to liberal expectations, anti-Semitism has proved to be the most durable ideology of the twentieth century. If we understand ideology in Raymond Aron's terms as combining an interpretation of history with a program of action "toward a future predicted or hoped for," only anti-Semitism among the major ideologies of modern Europe came close to achieving its stated aim, which was to rid the continent of Jews and Jewish influence. Despite the failure of movements with which it was sometimes closely aligned—Fascism on the one hand, Communism on the other—anti-Semitism *did* realize its vision of the future; and due to its proved success, it remains as vigorous and aggressive as ever, pursuing its program of action on another continent. Whereas Communism and Fascism spent their powers and came to an inglorious end, anti-Semitism arrived at the center of world politics with the United Nations as its pulpit.

Some people suspect that when Jews invoke anti-Semitism with regard to Israel they are trying either to absolve themselves of responsibility for their actions or justifying a hard line in politics. They think that anti-Semitism allows the Jews to magnify their importance or prove their innocence. In truth, however, it is demeaning for Jews to recognize that anti-Semitism may be the most important thing about them, and that they owe their standing at the center of modern history less to their own achievements than to the negative passions they inspire. Important as Jewish civilization may be for the balanced ethical life that it cultivates, and for the accomplishment of some of its members, Jews are also the most mythologized people on earth. And it is that mythology rather than their intrinsic nature that claims universal attention. One may or may not believe that God elected the Jews to be the carriers of His Law as it is written in the Bible, but there is no doubt that many modernizing nations elected the Jews to be the scapegoat for their rage, forcing Jews into the prism of their hatred and into the sights of their weapons.

Why is the success of anti-Semitism so rarely credited? After all, between 1939 and 1945 seven-tenths of Europe's Jews were destroyed; their property and goods were taken over by the Germans and resident nationals; and the millenial European-Jewish culture embodied in hundreds of vibrant communities was practically erased. In almost every European city where Jews once lived, the Jewish graveyards, when still standing, are much more populous than the local Jewish communities. And the global Jewish population, once estimated at 17 million, is after fifty years still about 4 million short of replacement level.

Yet despite the unparalleled success of anti-Semitism, few university departments of political science, sociology, history, or philosophy bother to analyze the single European political ideal of the past century that nearly realized its ends. Nor despite all the talk about the Holocaust and the erection of so many memorials and museums to commemorate the event is very much attention paid to the political idea that brought it about. It would be pleasant to believe that this eclipse has been accompanied by the disappearance of the phenomenon—that no one bothers to reexamine its achievement because it is no longer relevant. Just the opposite is true. Unwillingness to credit the political potency of anti-Semitism is the key to its resuscitation. It would appear that the need to deny anti-Semitism is as strong in those who do so as its attraction is strong in those who espouse it.

One of the main reasons the Nazis were able to destroy European Jewry was a lack of imaginative appreciation for their idea and inattention to their stated purpose. Disbelief, incredulity, and denial on the part of both victims and onlookers worked to the advantage of those who wanted to eradicate the Jews. There is hardly a survivor on record, from Elie Wiesel of the orthodox Hungarian Jewish community of Sighet to Primo Levi of the assimilated Italian community of Turin, who did not expose the function of denial in furthering the ideal of anti-Semitism. Rescued diaries of Jews who perished during the war and reflective memoirs of some who survived it all condemn (with varying degrees of rage and self-laceration) the failure to take ideological hatred seriously.

So much disbelief, incredulity, and denial on the part of so many cannot be ascribed to mere oversight. It must derive from something deeper—from an image of Man so different that it seems to preclude belonging to the same species. Those who define human beings as reasonable and rational creatures, kindly in their instincts and predisposed to peaceful coexistence, find anti-Semitism simply inconceivable. Jews who believe that people were fashioned in the image of God must consider anti-Semitism inhuman. If one tends to optimism and to ideas of progress like the liberals described in the previous chapter, such prejudice is inadmissible. This unwillingness to credit the strength of negative ideas means, in practice, that when anti-Semites ascribe their misery to the Jews and blame their godlessness on Jewish blasphemy, their poverty on Jewish greed, the decline of their cultural cohesion on the alien Jew in their midst, and their homelessness on the presence of a Jewish state, many would rather accept their excuses for hatred than face the enmity that generates them. To the degree that anti-Semitism threatens their cherished view of human nature, they will go to great lengths to deny it.

Materially, anti-Semitism targets only the Jew. But it cannot be curbed without the intervention of Gentiles—who invented it. Its defeat requires, on the part of both victims and onlookers, a temporary sacrifice of the liberal optimism upon which the whole of democratic society is founded. The stronger anti-Semitism grows, the more it forces a choice between defense of the Jews on the one hand and faith in the essential moderating reasonableness of human nature on the other. Small wonder that given the requirements for its containment, insufficient political support was mustered for the Jews in Europe. And this reluctance to defend the Jews had no small role in giving anti-Semites the confidence to persevere in their efforts.

What defeated other negative ideological movements of this century was the force of opposition ranged against them. Fascism, when it determined to conquer all of Europe, mobilized the resistance of the democratic west. Communism was defeated by the belated resistance of democratic countries to its expansion, by tenacious dissidents inside the Communist regimes, and perhaps most of all, by economic erosion. But the aggression of anti-Semitism against an absurdly small minority ensures that it cannot be countered by opposition in kind, and its singular focus on the Jews makes it irrelevant to those who are not Jews. Although the anti-Semite cannot call on the active participation of all onlookers, he can almost always count on their passive collusion. Indeed, the more virulent anti-Semitism grows, the more ordinary people are inclined to wish it away.

After the fact, too, many people continue to avoid a subject that is quite literally hateful. There are ethnic Poles, Ukrainians, Hungarians, Croatians, Austrians, as well as Germans who object to the study of anti-Semitism because they think it will expose weaknesses in their national history. They consider Jewish mourning itself a threat, since it seems to charge them implicitly with having been its cause. Already in 1966 the Auschwitz survivor Jean Amery (pseudonym of

Hans Mayer) described in an essay on "Resentment" how difficult it was to talk about German crimes in a world that could not tolerate the idea of collective guilt. "*I am burdened with collective guilt, I say; not they. The world, which forgives and forgets, has sentenced me, not those who murdered or allowed the murder to occur.*" For wanting to keep alive the memory of Auschwitz, Amery felt himself being turned into the morally condemnable Shylock, "but already cheated of the pound of flesh too." The world which forgives and forgets blames the survivor for bringing his discomfiting accusation back with him from the edge of the grave.

Philo-Semitic Gentiles or people with no pronounced sentiments about the Jews of any kind may be reluctant to confront the subject of Jew-hatred because they are worried about stirring up latent anti-Semitism in themselves or in others; because the cognitive separation of Jews seems to create artificial differences where there are none; or because they would rather work toward an improved future than recall the nadir of European civilization. Benign as this avoidance may seem, it perpetuates the choice of the Jew as target, since there are obviously good and valid causes for the success of anti-Semitism that can never be withstood unless they are first identified and understood. Jean Amery committed suicide, driven "to the mind's limits" and beyond by the dishonest postwar reimposition of normalcy. The Jews as a people are doubly threatened—by the brunt of anti-Semitism should they fail to anticipate its threat, and by the disaffection of their fellows when they do attend to it.

Ideological anti-Semitism consolidated in Germany in the

The Twentieth Century's Most Durable Ideology

late 1870s as part of a general growth of ideological movements. In his enlightening book on the history of modern
anti-Semitism, Jacob Katz explains the conditions surrounding the first use of the term. When the legal emancipation of
the Jews of Europe was almost complete, and separation of
church and state guaranteed equal rights to all citizens
irrespective of religion, there could be no further objection to
the advancement of Jews into the salons, the professions, the
arts, and all sectors of society. Since the Jews were equal
before the law, how could one justify opposition to their
progress? Anti-Semitism justifed its antipathy by accusing the
Jews of being unworthy of the rights to which they might
otherwise be entitled. Anti-Semitism distinguished itself
from anti-Jewishness—that is, from earlier opposition to the
Jewish religion—by claiming to oppose the Jews not because
of any bias but because Jewish racial characteristics, such as
their conspiratorial nature and their domineering ambition,
made them untrustworthy and a corrupting influence in the
emerging new liberal polities. Wilhelm Marr's 1879 pamphlet
The Victory of Judaism over Germanism, written in the form
of an eleventh-hour warning against a foreign influence that
had all but conquered Germany, proposed the formation of a
League of Anti-Semites that would unite all Germans in an
attempt to save the fatherland from "complete Judaization."
Marr introduced the word anti-Semitism into the political
vocabulary, and the movement that he initiated in Germany
had its counterpart in many other European countries
undergoing a similar painful transformation into modern
nationhood.

The negative image of the Jew as an undesirable anti-type,

taken over by modern nationalist movements from the Christian (and later the Muslim) religion, offered a strong thread of continuity between the eroding religious authority of the past and the emerging secular state. In Catholic countries like France and Poland, as well as in largely Protestant Germany, antipathy toward the Jews may have persisted while other religious rites and beliefs were being abandoned because the negative ideal of the Church satisfied deeper needs in some of its adherents than its positive teachings of grace and redemption. The received demonic image of the Jew when combined with his actual political vulnerability made him an ideal organizing target for dema-gogues who wanted to find a palpable explanation and tangible solution for complex social problems. Whipping up resentment against putatively privileged and corrupt groups has been a standard technique of both political authorities and challengers from the earliest times. Anti-Semitism proved a useful tool for both rulers and revolutionaries, since in most modern power struggles, Jews were equally expend-able to all the parties.

Because of their vulnerability, the Jews found no allies in Europe, not even in such opponents of anti-Semitism as the Marxists. Appealing as they did to the same disaffected elements in society, Marxists were forced to confront the rival force of anti-Semitism, which soon became one of the strongest features of Rightist politics. Yet, the attitude of Marxism toward the Jews was itself sufficiently troubling: The anti-Jewish animus of Karl Marx's 1844 essay "On the Jewish Question" had contributed significantly to the perpetuation of anti-Jewish prejudice, and certainly did nothing to stem it.

The Twentieth Century's Most Durable Ideology

But whatever their personal attitudes, the leaders of Marxist movements at the end of the century had to find a way of discrediting the anti-Semitic ideologues whom they faced at the polls by challenging the movement directly. Hence German Marxists, who confronted the most highly developed anti-Semitic movement on the continent, were in the forefront of the ideological battle against it.

To August Bebel, co-founder (with Wilhelm Liebknecht) of the German Social Democratic Party, is attributed the famous definition of anti-Semitism as "the socialism of fools." Unlike so many of the other socialist leaders and theoreticians in Germany, Bebel was not a Jew but the son of a Prussian noncommissioned army officer, which may have accounted for his very wide personal appeal as a labor leader and for his ability to assess popular anti-Semitism with the dispassionate eye of a practical politician. His epithet implied that the revolutionary impulse so intelligently developed by Marxism upon a closely argued theory of history was being stupidly misdirected by populist anti-Semites against an irrelevant target. After dealing with the problem for a number of years, Bebel proposed the following resolution on anti-Semitism at the Berlin Congress of the Social Democratic Party in 1893:

> Anti-Semitism springs from the discontent of certain bourgeois strata, who find themselves adversely affected by the development of capitalism and are, in part, destined to perish economically as a result of these trends. These groups, however, mistake the actual causes of their situation and therefore do not fight against the capitalist economic system, but against such surface phenomena appearing in it

which seem to hurt them most in the competitive struggle: namely, the Jewish exploiters.

Thus its origin obliges anti-Semitism to make demands that are as much in contradiction with the laws of capitalist economic and political development as they are hostile to progress. Hence also the support which anti-Semitism finds among Junkers and clerics.

The one-sided struggle of anti-Semitism against Jewish exploitation must necessarily remain without success, since the exploitation of man by man is not a specifically Jewish form of livelihood but one specific to bourgeois society, which will only end with the decline of bourgeois society.

Since social democracy is the most resolute foe of capitalism—whether its agents are Jews or Gentiles—and since it aims to eliminate bourgeois society by transforming it into a socialist society, thereby ending all domination of man by man, as well as all exploitation of man by man, social democracy refuses to divide its forces in the struggle against the existing State and social order by engaging in false and hence ineffective struggles against a symptom which stands and falls with bourgeois society.

Social democracy fights anti-Semitism as a movement which is directed against the natural development of society but which, despite its reactionary character and against its will, must ultimately become revolutionary. This is bound to happen because the petty bourgeois and small peasant strata, which are being whipped up by anti-Semitism against the Jewish capitalists, will finally realize that not merely the Jewish capitalists, but the capitalist class as a whole, is its enemy. Hence only the fulfilment of socialism can free them from their misery.

This resolution's opposition to anti-Semitism is as unequivocal as its faith in historical determinism; but that is precisely why it would accommodate and leave intact the thing it opposed. (Anti-Semitism is attacked not for the harm it does to Jews but for the energy it saps from Marxism.) In the first place, Bebel's diagnosis had nothing to do with the illness. Like a clergyman who prescribes faith for someone seeking a cure for cancer, the Marxist's diagnosis of anti-Semitism was materially irrelevant, brutally irrelevant, to the condition it purported to alleviate. The eschatological rhetoric of Bebel's declaration—"destined to perish," "must necessarily remain," "must ultimately become," "is bound to happen," "will finally realize"—is the product of a mind so fixed in its certainties that it cannot entertain the possibility of an honest struggle between its own laws that are deemed to be *natural* and a political movement it has already written off. This is the more unfortunate since not a word of Bebel's analysis was true. Anti-Semitism did not spring from the discontent of certain bourgeois strata with the development of capitalism, but from a combination of fears, frustrations, historical memories, idealism, and much else, whose complex role in human affairs the Marxist theory of historical determinism did much to obscure. Anti-Semitic groups were not opposed to the Jewish exploiters in any specific economic sense, but (as any clear-eyed reader of anti-Semitic literature could attest) also to Jewish artists, journalists, musicians, and purveyors of ideas, including the Jewish advocates of Marxism. That anti-Semitism was hostile to what Bebel calls progress is correct, of course, but he failed to note that from their own point of view anti-Semites felt they were defending their civilization against the progress of barbarism and preserving their familiar way of life against "foreign" attempts to undermine it. In misdefining anti-Semitism, Marxists perpetuated an intellectual error, retarding attempts to understand it for what it was.

Furthermore, many Marxists tacitly endorsed anti-Semitism when they failed to condemn its specific attack against the Jews. Marxism triggered a politics of hatred directed against an abstract class, then tried to teach its troops, the proletariat, to distinguish between a Jewish capitalist and an abstract one. Anti-Semitism was more straightforward, wanting a clear and tactile representation of the "class" it hated. Since revolutionary Marxism promoted opposition to human beings not in response to their individual behavior but for the crime of belonging to a social category, it could hardly attack anti-Semitism on moral grounds for similarly lashing out against a group, irrespective of its members' deeds. Note that to call anti-Semitism, as Bebel does, "the socialism of fools" implies no moral condemnation. Similarly, Bebel's resolution on anti-Semitism makes no objection to it on moral grounds, since he is no less eager than the anti-Semites to foment revolution by turning different groups against each another. Indeed, Bebel's emphasis on the error rather than the immorality of anti-Semitism implicitly acknowledges that the movements of the Right and Left are otherwise politically related in their means, while the failure to defend Jews for their own sake implies that Jewishness is of no independent value. To the degree that Bebel was expressing views characteristic of his Marxist contemporaries—views that precluded a defense of the Jews because it sought their disappearance by other means—one might want to ask whether socialism was not the anti-Semitism of intellectuals.

Marxism appreciated the aggressive energy of anti-Semitism but tried to shift or to broaden the target without condemning the impulse—and without defending the Jews as Jews. For their part, liberal intellectuals and politicians were also slow in coming to the explicit defense of the Jews despite their genuine abhorrence of the implied violence of both movements. To stand up to anti-Semitism meant abandoning the political vocabulary of the greatest thinkers in order to concentrate on plain political aggression against a single group. It also meant entering the fray at the lowest and ugliest level. Many ideological liberals were unsympathetic to the fate of the Jews, not because of any personal antipathy but because the national fate of the Jews contradicted their view of the world and called into question their deepest assumptions. It goes without saying that the ranks of these ideological liberals, like the ranks of the Marxists, were replete with Jews seeking an escape from the negative role in which they were being cast.

Thus far, we have drawn attention to the purposefulness of anti-Semitism and to some of the reasons for its political success. How do the Jews figure in this process? Is it true, as many Gentiles believe, that Jews exploit anti-Semitism for their own political ends and try to exaggerate its importance in order to portray themselves as victims? Woody Allen's comical observation that even paranoiacs have enemies evokes nervous laughter in Jews who know how hard it is to distinguish on a daily basis between an enmity that warrants attention and mere unpopularity. Because of the way anti-Semitism distorts and magnifies, it is very hard to see the Jews as they really are, for themselves as well as others. Without an accurate political assessment of the Jews, however, anti-Semitism can never be effectively curbed.

Far from exploiting anti-Semitism, Jews have actually been notoriously slow to confront its reality. During two thousand years of exile from their land for what they believed was God's dissatisfaction with them, Jews tried to atone through prayer and study and observance of His commandments. As long as they were wrapped up in the great drama of their contractual service to God, Jews considered their behavior and their fate to be of ultimate significance, whether or not it was appreciated by the other nations of the world, and accordingly they interpreted the attacks upon them as part of a divine plan. By contrast, when modern Jews who no longer considered themselves subject to God found themselves facing the hatred of anti-Semites, they felt unspeakably degraded with nothing to gain from being thus singled out.

It is humiliating to stand subject to the will of your moral inferiors knowing that they wield over you the power of life and death. Jews were far more interested in proving themselves acceptable to their new fellow citizens than worrying about the "misconceptions" of their detractors. While traditional Jews could avoid the indignity of anti-Semitism by continuing to look to the Lord of Hosts as their protector, many modern Jews were not even certain they wanted to maintain a Jewish identity, much less in the face of ugly provocation. In order to appreciate the political attraction of anti-Semitism, which is the first condition for containing it, Jews would have had to study the mind of their inspired enemies the way they had historically debated the will of God. For Jews to engage in such an inquiry would have meant confronting the humiliation of hatred instead of trusting in eventual acceptance. It would have meant trading in the eschatological optimism of the messianic dream for the political pragmatism of defending against extinction. Even then, it is doubtful whether they could have mustered the political power necessary to quell the powers ranged against them.

Let us look at this process through a specific historical example—not through the darkest prism of Germany or Poland but through the marginally less gruesome experience of Russian Jews over the past century. Following the assassination of Czar Alexander II in 1881, his successors whipped up anti-Jewish feeling to redirect the dissatisfaction of the masses away from the government. This policy not only discriminated against Jews as members of another religion but deliberately fashioned them into a political scapegoat, and through such provocations as the *Protocols of the Elders of Zion* tried to spread the news among the Russian people that the Jews were an enemy within, a state within a state. Nationalist bands were armed and encouraged to incite spontaneous pogroms on the government's behalf.

Thus, as favored victims of the czars, Jews might have been expected to benefit the most from the Bolshevik Revolution of 1917, an enforced social overhaul that among other achievements abolished the absolutist monarchy and outlawed anti-Semitism. This expectation, indeed, is what finally reconciled many younger Jews to the Communist system after the Revolution, despite initial widespread Jewish distrust of the Bolsheviks. The presumed benefit to the Jews is also what associated them in the popular imagination with the newly imposed regime.

But while many Jews tried to adapt to Communism, Communism could not tolerate the Jews, an unassimilable minority with national ties to people in other lands, including democratic countries. Bebel's early Marxist ideas prepare us for the ever-hardening opposition of Communism to the independent survival of the Jews as a people. When Stalin tightened his control over Russia as the csars had done with their subjects, he too found in the Jew the ideal political scapegoat. His post-World War II campaigns against "rootless cosmopolitans" and "bourgeois nationalists" placed Jews under a double burden of hatred: perceived by many Russians as enforcers of the system, they found themselves identified by the Communist dictator as enemies of the system.

No wonder, then, that in the 1960s and 1970s Jews were disproportionately active among Soviet dissidents, for Jews stood to benefit the most from any liberalization that might be effected, let alone from an actual breakup of the regime. Some expectations of improvement were eventually fulfilled: Jews were given permission to study Hebrew, to engage in religious rituals, to emigrate. Yet as soon as Communism weakened, one of the first freedoms claimed by Russians and other nationals was—the freedom to oppose the Jews. The slogan of the Moldavian nationalist movement of the late 1980's, "We will drown the Communists in the blood of the Jews," is a localized update of the much older motto, "Bury the Jews and save Russia." Thus instead of being hailed as defiant pioneers who helped crack the totalitarian yoke, Jews in the former Soviet Union today are perceived as a threat to the cohesion of almost every discrete nationalist unit. After three strikes, many Russian Jews in the Soviet Union are calling themselves out and heading for Israel.

To that extent they are redeeming the promise of Zionism. For Zionism aspired to save Jews from the persecution to which they were subjected as a minority by returning them to their own land where they could rule themselves. Yet instead of changing the fate of the Jews, Israel has assumed the fate of the Jews. The Arab and Muslim countries of the Middle East, in their opposition to the Jewish state and the idea of a Jewish nation, have discovered the same political opportunities that inspired so many other modernizing European peoples. Already during World War II—which the Mufti of Jerusalem spent in Berlin, urging Hitler not to overlook any Jewish children in his campaign of destruction—the transition was forged between the most virulent form of European anti-Semitism and its Arab successor. Whatever else the Russian Jews will find in Israel, they will not be granted refuge from Jew-hatred.

The repetitiveness of the Jewish condition is positively boring, so boring that the temptation of denial can hardly be resisted. Faced with a protean anti-Semitism that can combine with so many other political movements, even the sturdiest Jews grow reluctant to resist it, whether on their own behalf or on behalf of fellow Jews. This reluctance grows out of weariness, a sense of sacrificed dignity and squandered energy that dulls the pleasure of life itself.

We say that love is blind, implying that the lover blinds *himself* to flaws in his beloved that he might ordinarily be expected to see. Blind hatred works in a different way, obscuring the impulses of the hater while magnifying a thousandfold the flaws in the one despised. Where the lover is content to languish in dreams, the hater is hyperactive, boiling over with destructive energy. And this energy in the hater saps the energy of his target, adding injury to the insult of being hauled into the court of someone else's opinion.

Unilateral hatred can only be withstood if it is challenged with sufficient force. But how can the victim of such hatred mount a sufficient counterattack if he lacks the instinct of reciprocal aggression? What usually happens is that the exhaustion of the victim stimulates the dynamism of his predator in an accelerating cycle.

Jew-hatred further undermines the moral strength of the Jews by attributing to them something they are not. Anti-Semites charge the Jews with bloodthirstiness and vengeance, citing the Bible's *lex talionis*—an eye for an eye, a tooth for a tooth—and the way stern justice is administered in biblical Israel's military conquests. They charge the Jews with exclusiveness and racism, referring to the Jews' claim to be the chosen people. Actually, however, postbiblical Judaism pacified the Bible almost to the point of inversion, multiplying laws of self-discipline at the expense of retaliatory concepts and judgments. For crimes deserving capital punishment the rabbis made evidentiary requirements so stringent that they effectively inactivated the death penalty. Jews did continue to set themselves apart from other people, but with the implicit understanding that anyone who wished to could become a

The Twentieth Century's Most Durable Ideology

Jew. Nor did anything in Judaism correspond to the Christian and Muslim resentment of the Jew as the denier of *their* faiths; consequently, nothing in Jewish history corresponds to the spasms of Christian and Muslim anti-Semitism.

The resulting asymmetry between Jews and anti-Jews creates a perpetual political imbalance. My late teacher, the Yiddish linguist Max Weinreich, once traced for me the following history of the Yiddish term *hargenen,* "to kill." Enjoying no active use among the Jews of Europe, the term gradually acquired the weaker meaning of "strike," or "beat," while to signify real killing one said *derhargenen,* employing a prefix for an action seen through to its end. But this stronger term, too, came to mean no more than "beat," or "rough up," and for killing one resorted to *derhargenen oyf toyt*—to kill to death.

My teacher presented this item of moral philology in a spirit of obvious respect for the linguistic community that spawned it, a community which had lost the habit of killing. This was the same Max Weinreich, educated at the University of Marburg, who right after the war wrote *Hitler's Professors,* a book documenting the early and widespread pro-Hitler sentiment in the German academic community and the creative participation of some of the finest German minds, including a number of Nobel laureates, in the Final Solution. One wonders whether Weinreich ever considered the fit between what he knew about Jews and what he knew about Germans. But assuming that he was as right about the one as the other, how could people so disinclined to kill expect to survive among people who so enjoyed the prospect? And to what extent might the pacific civilization of the Jews have provoked the anti-Semitism of Germans and Russians? Did the bleat of the lamb excite the tiger?

As opposed to what one might call normally competitive ideas and movements, anti-Semitism unleashes a unilateral energy of enmity. Though lacking in philosophical heft, it is special among political instruments and ideas by dint of its vigor. When Hannah Arendt reported on the trial of Adolf Eichmann in 1961 in her much debated book *Eichmann in Jerusalem,* she discovered a man so pedestrian and stupid that he literally could not lie to save his life, a robotic state functionary fully illustrating her thesis of the "banality of evil." But Cynthia Ozick is at least equally correct when she asserts that for sheer creativity no modern poetic metaphor can match the showers designed by Germans to cleanse Jews of their lives. The Nazis solved their Jewish problem with considerable ingenuity, and had Eichmann not risen so inventively to his task, the Jews would still be "polluting" Europe with their presence rather than fertilizing it with their ashes. Arendt would have done better to respect the adaptive capacities of the anti-Jewish idea, rather than note the dullness of its representatives once their passions were spent.

To be sure, anti-Semitism has triggered tremendous bursts of energy in modern Jews as well. But as already said, the main thrust of Jewish energy has been to gain acceptance, including in the nations eager to be rid of them. The dynamism of the Jews in the nineteenth and twentieth centuries is unique. No other people migrated in such proportion to their overall numbers, or rerooted themselves so successfully in their new homes. Wherever Jews were permitted to flourish, and occasionally where they were not, they manifested a creative as opposed to a destructive energy, and perhaps tried to compensate for their handicaps by spectacular achievements. Having no desire to engage their adversaries, they tried to prove themselves unworthy of hatred.

All this sounds exemplary, and so it may be, but since anti-Semitism bears no relation to the achievement of the Jews it cannot be dispelled by proofs of their excellence. Jew-hatred is one-sided, not only in the sense that it is unreciprocated but in the sense that it functions independently of its object. Jews could dispel anti-Semitism through their behavior only if it were directed against their behavior. But given that the fear and hatred derive from the accuser himself, and are often a projection of his own desires, they can only be dispelled by a revision in his mind. To put it in contemporary political terms: were Arab opposition to a Jewish nation based on the quality of that nation, on something correctable in Jewish policies, Israel could aspire to satisfy it. But the Arab charge that Israel is racist by definition supersedes and remains invulnerable to proof.

Anti-Semitism sets all kinds of traps for its victims. The Jew may think he can turn hatred to advantage. A handicapped person in learning to compensate for his disability often outperforms the normal person in other ways. But just as the handicapped person may eventually tire of the special exertions required of him, so too may the Jew under the disability of hatred. Israel's intelligence agency Mossad, for example, may have become one of the outstanding secret services in the world because Israel had to compensate through its Intelligence for its relative political, demographic, geographic, and economic disadvantages. But the Mossad cannot be expected to protect Israel forever from Arab plots to destroy it. Should Jews continue to require more and more of themselves rather than more and more of their enemies, they would simply be continuing the game of hounds and hares instead of demanding an end to the cruel sport.

Exhaustion breeds another fantasy: the Jew is tempted to try to elicit from bystanders and witnesses the same pity he feels for himself. Thus in misguided effort, some American Jewish organizations have encouraged the teaching of the Holocaust to Gentiles, just as Israeli statesmen take their Gentile visitors to the Holocaust memorial of Yad Vashem. They expect that imparting information about the murder of the Jews of Europe will ensure its never happening again. Yet almost everything we know about human nature and history would lead to a more obvious conclusion. From the images of Auschwitz and Buchenwald one could derive that: (a) Jews are an easy target; (b) something must be wrong with the Jews if they were selected as a target; (c) it is not a good idea to be a Jew. Since innocence was not a shield against destruction in the first place, it is hard to see how advertising innocence will do any better.

Some of the most intellectually gifted modern Jews have tried to escape the humiliation of Jew-hatred by transforming both the aggression and their defense against it into a higher principle. Just note the conspicuous role played by the "Jewish question" in the search for universal theories of human behavior and in movements aimed at political re-demption. Written at the beginning of his career, Karl Marx's essay "On the Jewish Question" insisted that "the social emancipation of the Jews is the emancipation of society from Judaism," making it clear just how high were his hopes that the political evolution of Europe would preclude any further need for Jewish survival. Historian Robert Wistrich, who specializes in the history of assimilating Jewry of Germany and Austria-Hungary, documents the efforts of a wide assortment of Jewish geniuses to transpose their loyalties from nation to class. In their own estimation these idealists were attempting to improve the condition of mankind as a whole, which is perforce a nobler ambition than merely securing the Jews. But the move into the embrace of mankind was a process of assimilation that would eliminate the Jews along with the need to defend them.

The need to transcend the discomfort of anti-Semitism played a part in the social theorizing of thinkers as different as Sigmund Freud, the founder of psychoanalysis, and Franz Boas, the pioneer of anthropology, and in the practical attempt of Ludwig Zamenhoff to create an international language, Esperanto, so that human beings would be brought closer together in mutual understanding. Noam Chomsky's theories about transformational grammar are linked in a similarly complex way to his father's occupation as a scholar of Hebrew. It would be hard to explain the obsessive preoccupations of this universalizing linguist with the evils of the *Jewish* state of Israel except as an expression of anger with the Jews for remaining so indissolubly untransformed, and as part of a sublimating attempt to get beyond the condition of Jewish specificity once and for all.

These and other Jewish geniuses obviously produced much that was of independent and universal value. In reality, however, the "Jewish question" was the question of anti-Semitism, which could only be addressed through an analysis of the particular ideology of hatred, and could only be eradicated through the unambiguous acceptance of actual Jews. Transmuting Jew-hatred into the larger issue of society was the intellectual equivalent of social climbing, of trying to dissociate oneself from the despised minority while reaching for ideas of power. Not only did these theories leave existing anti-Semitism untouched and intact, they sometimes contributed—most notably in Marxism—a new set of reasons for eliminating the Jews.

The latest attempt to avoid or transcend Jew-hatred by subsuming it under a broader category is the umbrella movement for human rights, under which many Jews have tried to find shelter. The Jewish human-rights activists I know have almost nothing in common with the earlier socialist-internationalist opponents of Jewish peoplehood, being genuinely concerned with the defense of Judaism, of Israel, and of the Jews. But they, too, wish to transcend parochialism by defending the rights of all people everywhere. They justify this on tactical as well as moral grounds, arguing that a broad-based approach is necessary since it can mobilize a larger following, attract more publicity, hence prove more effective. The argument overlooks just one detail—the opportunity the Jew-hater will find in each new general principle to exclude from it his designated enemy.

A local example from my university is typical: To commemorate the achievement of the struggle for Soviet Jewry, the Montreal Jewish community established in the McGill Faculty of Law a lecture series in human rights, named for one of the heroes of that struggle, Natan Sharansky. A lecture series in *Jewish* law might have been more to the point. Such a series could have made at least a small contribution to knowledge by tracing the contemporary politics of Jewish rescue back to its sources. But since the goal of the struggle for Soviet Jewry had been a human-rights goal, the organizers skipped over the means and hastened right to the end. Sharansky himself had always interpreted his personal battle to be allowed to emigrate to Israel as part of the larger fight for personal liberty under Communism, and in that sense nothing could have honored him more appropriately than a lecture series on human rights. But already by the third year of the series, a proposal was introduced for a lecture on Israel's abuse of the rights of Palestinian Arabs.

The Arab propounders of this idea cared as much about human rights as the Communists before them cared about world peace. However, they had learned to conceal their aims by resorting to the same language the Jews were trying to grasp for their protection. Thus can a general principle like "human rights" serve the double purpose of furthering anti-Jewish propaganda while depriving Jews of one of their moral props. Feeling so good about the struggle they had presumably won, the Jews of Montreal ignored the political war being waged against their people and handed their enemy a brand new weapon. Now, if the donors of the lectures were to withdraw their support to prevent the foreseeable subversion of their aims, they will be accused of having contempt for human rights—and no doubt, of censorship as well.

Modern Jews have enthusiastically fought for the civil and human rights of other persecuted minorities, convinced that a threat to any group is a threat to them. It is almost unbearably discouraging for the Jews to admit that other minorities, including other persecuted minorities, do not share their conviction but, to the contrary, discover in anti-Semitism a handy political tool of their own. In Europe, anti-Semitism was often the common denominator of the poorest and richest sectors of society, and its usefulness in this regard has not been lost on some Americans either. Anti-Semitism is the glue of the unlikely alliance that appears to be developing between some blacks and Arabs, both locally and internationally; the anticipated economic benefits of such an alliance seem to count for more among those who enter into it than the genuineness of Jewish involvement with their cause.

And so it goes, on and on and on. Before so relentless an assault, many good people are tempted to ask, "Why does everyone hate the Jews?" as though anti-Semitism were one of the eternal mysteries, beyond analysis or correction. This attribution of anti-Semitism to a realm beyond human understanding or control may be the most dangerous trap of all, since its capitulation to despair guarantees inaction. Actually, the question is fraudulent, since "everyone" does not "hate" the Jews. In the United States today, in particular, Jews continue to prosper and to play a prominent part in every area of society; and despite the resurgence of anti-Semitism in certain circles, it continues to be regarded as a disreputable sentiment achieving a certain legitimacy only when it travels under the cover of anti-Zionism. The emphasis on "everyone" is dangerous because it obscures the particular goals of those who really do hate the Jews and who profit from Jew-hatred.

In contending with so relentless an assault many Jews grow weary, and the very mention of anti-Semitism draws a yawn. Yet the weariness must be overcome, as much for the sake of the world as for the safety of the Jews. The only way to overcome it is to resist the seductive temptations of the universalist illusion and to engage in the defense of that very particularity against which the ideology of anti-Semitism has always been at war.

Chapter Three

A Light unto the Nations?

When Moses Hess took up the subject of the Jews in his 1862 book *Rome and Jerusalem,* he wrote in the form of letters of condolence to an unnamed woman in mourning. To ease her bereavement, he assures his friend that he has decided to return to his people, "to be one of them again, to participate in the celebration of the holy days, to share the memories and hopes of the nation, to take part in the spiritual and intellectual warfare going on within the House of Israel, on the one hand, and between our people and the surrounding, civilized, nations on the other." He implies that the return of a Jew to his people could compensate another Jew for her loss of kin. The unnamed woman in mourning cannot help but evoke Lamentation's haunting image of conquered Jerusalem:

If I Am Not For Myself

How doth the city sit solitary,
That was full of people!
How is she become as a widow!
She that was great among the nations,
And princess among the provinces,
How is she become tributary!

Trying to raise the fallen spirits of his fellow Jews, Hess went far beyond condolence in his vision of a reconstituted modern Jewish nation.

Moses Hess (1812–1875) was the first European intellectual to recognize that as a member of the family of nations in a period of emerging nation states, the Jews, too, would have to refashion their homeland Eretz Yisrael. His pioneering Zionism was the more unusual since Hess had earlier been one of the pioneers of Communism, first a mentor and then a huge admirer of Karl Marx, and the man who instructed Friedrich Engels. For his promotion of socialism through violent rebellion in the newspaper *Rheinische Zeitung* Hess was accused of having fathered radical Communism in Germany and forced to flee for his life to France. Dubbed "the Red rabbi," he continued to believe throughout his life in a classless society and in its steady improvement through the applied findings of the social and natural sciences.

But Hess parted company with the scientific socialism of Marx and Engels, recognizing that Communism undervalued other aspects of human development, especially national-cultural considerations, to a degree that undermined its

truth. He was moved to pity not only by the exploitation of
the working class, but by the suffering of his fellow Jews who
were pauperized and persecuted both in Europe and the
Middle East. By contrast, the progress toward the unification
of Italy under the liberal banner of Garibaldi and Mazzini
gave him the idea that the Jews would be able to surmount
their difficulties if they followed a similar road to national
self-emancipation. The political philosopher and historian
Sir Isaiah Berlin notes that Hess "turned out to have a deeper
understanding of some essential matters than more gifted and
sophisticated social thinkers."

Hess seems to have discovered Zionism quite on his own,
in the course of rejecting the racism of conservative Germans
and the ideological anti-Semitism of European revolutionaries. The homey, unsystematic thrust of his argument pro-
motes the cause of a revitalized nation in the organic imagery
of seeds and flowers rather than in the capitalized abstractions
favored by his German philosophical contemporaries. When
he speaks of the human family, he explains that his image of
it grows straight from his mother's love, which is not only the
emotional but the fructifying intellectual origin of his own
love for mankind:

> Judaism has never drawn any line of separation between
> the individual and the family, the family and the nation, the
> nation and humanity as a whole, humanity and the cosmos,
> nor between the creation and the Creator. . . . Judaism is
> rooted in the love of the family; patriotism and nationalism
> are the flowers of its spirit, and the coming regenerated state
> of human society will be its ripe fruit.

Many a Jewish teacher demonstrates to his students that all men are brothers by drawing a stick figure of the biblical Adam at the top of a page and a geometric progression of his offspring beneath. In the same way, Hess is convinced that the Jewish idea of loving wholeness—whose highest philosophical interpreter he believes to be Spinoza—can inspire the fraternal reform of all human society.

From his innocent enthusiasm about this project one can hardly guess that Hess was trying to defuse an explosive idea. He knew that this view of the Jews as an organic family had begun to gain threatening force in Europe. The robust family of his description was perceived by others as a conspiring clan, like the ubiquitous Rothschilds who were building their international banking empire across otherwise divided frontiers. "The German hates the Jewish religion less than the race," Hess wrote with unnerving sobriety. "He objects less to the Jews' peculiar beliefs than to their peculiar noses." Even after the Jew had done everything to accommodate himself to the surrounding majority—shaved his beard, adopted local dress, mastered German, proved himself an outstanding musician/philosopher/businessman—the Germans still objected that he was only trying to camouflage his essential and ineradicable Jewishness.

Nothing daunted by this accusation, Hess cheerfully agreed that the Jews could never become good Germans. The Germans' abstract passion for "pure human nature" was really an excuse to seek domination over all other races, and made *them* the most dangerous people in Europe. As for the French, who had struggled for liberty, equality, fraternity, they represented to Hess the ideal of brotherhood. Then there was Italy, which inspired Hess with a model for the resurrection of Jerusalem. But it was the idea of a deeply ethical modern Jewish nation that nurtured his optimism about nationalism in general.

And buoyant he was, the sunny forecaster of a reawakened people that would rebuild its homeland in the land of Israel. Many nice people of Europe were mistakenly trying to establish closer ties among all the nations of the world by denying the typical, creative characteristic of each. Against this destructive uniformity he appealed to the original organic community—the Jews—to demonstrate that nationalism was not only compatible with humanism but a guarantor against the leveling tendencies of technology and conformism.

To Hess, the history of the Jews proved that nations were not so easily dissoluble, and that the moral energy of their survival was a force for good, not evil. As a child he had seen his grandfather, in the synagogue, mourning the destruction of the ancient temple in Jerusalem, and had heard him pray for the return of the Jews to Zion. He had been told the story of Mother Rachel weeping at her tomb in Hebron when the soldiers of Nebuchadnezzar drove the children of Israel into exile after destroying the holy city. This parental love had sustained the children of Israel through centuries of dispersion and ensured their eventual return. Hess was an idealist: he championed the restoration of the Jewish state less as a practical antidote to European anti-Semitism than as the harbinger of a variegated world community.

Even at this historical remove the letters of *Rome and Jerusalem* are an inspiring example of intellectual independence. The courage it took to stand up to Karl Marx on one flank and the German-Jewish reformers on the other—to the radicals and liberals of his day who were also his peers and his friends—was as rare a century ago as it is today. Yet there is also something disquieting about Hess's mixture of politics and metaphysics, especially when applied to a people already the subject of too much mystification. The quality of national character can have nothing to do with a nation's right to exist, and unless you are God, the argument for a national homeland dare not be made on grounds of national merit.

I think one can understand how the two became fused in the mind of someone like Moses Hess, who had for a long time been under the exclusive influence of Western European thought, and who was stung by the assumptions of German superiority. Ashamed of having once judged his own culture by the standard of those who wanted only to destroy it, and freshly convinced of the moral grandeur of Jewish civilization, he wanted to reveal the power of the Jewish national idea. He had also to make his fellow Jews appreciate the worth of their own culture if they were to embrace their legitimate national existence. The admirability of Jewish achievement was hence offered as evidence of Jewish national legitimacy—a fatal mixture, since it appeared to make the legitimacy contingent on the admirability.

This remains the Jewish humanist's—and in this case the Jewish socialist's—very special, very deadly temptation. Once he feels, or regains, a measure of national confidence he tends to be so dazzled by his moral force that he would just as soon be judged on his merits as accepted for an equal. He does not believe in the religious basis of Jewish election, but in a secular echo of its special claims, he tries to prove his moral prowess instead of demanding his due. He is like the son of a murdered tightrope walker who insists on waiving the net to prove his nerve, forgetting that his father was killed not through lack of skill but by the rival who cut the rope. Nowadays, the Jewish moral strut is the specialty of those who want to prove the moral refinement of Israel before putting an end to the Arab war against it. You can see it performed every day in Washington and Jerusalem, in Paris and Buenos Aires.

Here is a small example to which I was witness. A group of Jews is talking tennis, and the conversation gets around to Israel's Davis Cup win over Czechoslovakia. After expressions of satisfaction with the rising level of Israel's tennis performance, speculation passes to the next round of play that is to take place in India. India, however, true to its long-standing anti-Israel foreign policy, had already refused Israel admission a year earlier when it had hosted the table-tennis tournament. Would India now honor its Davis Cup commitment or scandalously insult the Jewish state once again? At this point (and observe it carefully, because this is the key move of the moral strut) focus is shifted from India's discrimination to Israel's opportunity. Someone in the group suggests that Israel should have spared India embarrassment by agreeing to play in a third "neutral" country, thereby demonstrating to the world that Jews are above its petty politics.

Did you catch this Jewish sleight of hand, the almost imperceptible shift of scrutiny from the moral failings of others to the putative moral strength of the Jews? The discussion was about sport, whose charm is the guaranteed equality of rules within which individuals or teams can compete. Suddenly we are brought up short and reminded that even in this charmed sphere the Jewish state is not guaranteed equality. India panders to Arab hatred of Israel and to its own Muslim minority by excluding Israel whenever it can (to no great international outcry), admitting it only when faced with disqualification. Israel is singled out for the crime of its existence and made to test the principles of equality on which international sport, like international law, depend. But certain Jews are prepared to turn discrimination into a test of Israel, a chance to show off the vaunted Jewish moral superiority.

For an example of this maneuver on a grander scale, consider the aftermath of the massacres at the Palestinian camps of Sabra and Shatila in September 1982. On the facts of the massacre itself there seems to be agreement: while Israeli troops were still in Lebanon, Christian militiamen killed 460 people, about half of them women and children, in the two refugee camps near Beirut. It needs to be said that the slaughter was in retaliation for earlier massacres by Palestinian terrorists, and that these terrorists deliberately placed women and children in their military bases as a tactic of moral intimidation. But no provocations by the PLO could justify the militia's hand-to-hand killing of civilians, and the ensuing swell of outrage in the West was a reasonable expression of its disgust.

Israelis may have felt a special horror. These marauding Lebanese Christians were, after all, the potential "ally" of Israel in the peace settlement it had been seeking in the Middle East and its real military ally during the 1982 attempt to uproot the Palestinian bases from Lebanon. One had had higher hopes than this for Christian forces. There was also the troubling question of indirect responsibility. If the Israelis were in temporary military control of the area in which the massacre occurred, they had to wonder about sins of omission, a failure to foresee and to prevent it.

But others had actually committed the murders. Whatever happened to the killers? Did anyone put a price on their heads or make a serious effort to apprehend them? Why were they not hunted down so that they might be brought to trial and given the punishment they deserved? If the outrage was so great and the crime so brutal, where was the call for justice?

In truth, there was no moral outrage and no desire for retribution. The massacre was morally interesting only as a moment of reckoning with the Jews, an opportunity to apply that tired but still vigorous double standard that insists on monitoring the Jews for their purity so that they would be "more Catholic than the Pope." As soon as the government of Israel agreed to investigate its failure to prevent the massacres, real evil was welcome to run free.

I am not suggesting that Israel be held responsible for the escape of the murderers—as others wanted to hold it responsible for the murders themselves. Yet who can deny that the publicized inquiry into Israeli complicity helped to obscure the traces of the killers and the cycle of violence that continues? Israel, instead of demanding that its own inquiry be linked to a serious pursuit of the murderers, instead of asking Christians and Muslims to see to *their* morality, responded to the accusation of criminality by providing a convenient diversion, agreeing to stand alone in the dock. "I am glad to be held to a higher standard," says the moral supremacist, as though his morality rather than theirs was the legitimate concern of the nations of the world. As though even the highest standard of Jewish behavior could be a substitute for the decency of others. The transference to the international arena of a people's desire for holiness is a tragic mistake with potentially tragic consequences. By assuming even a fraction of the guilt that is not rightly his, the moral supremacist betrays the cause of righteousness in which he says he labors.

There is an obvious connection between the Jewish moral strut and what we have earlier defined as liberalism, but for the moment it is the Jewish version of the maneuver that concerns me. The insistence on equal justice for all would be met in certain Jewish circles with a chorus of *disapproval*: "Don't *you* believe that Jews ought to aspire to exemplary morality?" "Why, in fact, should we not hold the Jewish state to a higher standard of behavior?" "Aren't we supposed to be a 'light unto the nations'?" Strutters do not appear to recognize the difference between moral striving (the direction of which, in politics even more than in private life, is always open to debate) and political scapegoating. In politics it is not God who holds Israel to a double standard, but fellow states. Jewish morality is no more able to win over the enemy than Jewish immorality ever occasioned his enmity in the first place. Yet the moral strutters think they recognize a continuity between the Jew's election to carry the burden of the Law at Sinai and the choice of the modern Jew as a prime target of international discrimination. Their confusion of political villainy with God's claim on the Jews, and of anti-Israel coalitions with the Jewish striving for righteousness, actually abets evil and delays any possibility of international peace and justice.

Unfortunately, this attitude has deep roots. It has been with us since modern Jewish thinkers began to ascribe to their ideologies the same claims to election they had formerly professed as devout Jews. Moses Hess, for example, could not accept religious election as the continuing source of Jewish morality, because he no longer believed in a God of revelation or in a God Who mattered. At the same time, his respect for Jewish civilization—for the consequences of the Jewish contract with God through the millenia—made him eager to preserve his people's historical mission. The Jews mattered even if God did not. So he tried to identify the moral core of Jewishness with the emergent socialist faith in an egalitarian, responsible state that would be a new earthly example to the nations.

The resulting idea of Jewishness, when undertaken by someone as richly endowed as Hess with sensitivity, sympathy, and knowledge, could be morally persuasive and, for one generation at least, even culturally satisfying. But there are serious flaws in the argument. As long as the Jewish claim to election had rested on the Jew's acceptance of *Halakhah*, a prescribed way of life that derives from the granting of the Law at Sinai, it was open to all people alike. The Torah was a "tree of life" to all who clung to it, and everyone prepared to cling to it could become a Jew. Ruth the Moabite serves as the model for all proselytes to Judaism, who are invited to recognize a sign of their authenticity as Jews in the divine promise that the messiah himself will descend from her lineage.

But how, other than through Jewish birth, can you become a *Jewish* socialist or a *Jewish* humanist? And if you cannot *become* a Jewish socialist, is it not a form of racism to claim that Jewish socialists or a Jewish socialist state are potentially "a light unto the nations"? Do Jewish socialist parents in Israel or elsewhere teach their children that they are expected to be more moral than French or Danish socialists? In any case, if their ethics derive from a political program, then the program rather than the accident of their birth must be the source of their moral education and hence the determinant of their moral actions. The rational basis of socialism precludes any claim for any special moral striving of the Jews.

With one apparent exception—when Jews are singled out for mistreatment. The idealistic young Jewish reformers who opposed the autocratic abuses of the czarist regime in Russia, Moses Hess who defended the Jews against the Teutonic will to crush them cloaked themselves and their politics in the biblical language of prophetic righteousness, in the belief that their fight as underdogs against repressive authority obviously perpetuated the core values of the Jewish religious tradition. The contemporary Jews discussing the politics of tennis see the same pattern at work when India discriminates against the Jewish state. But the parallels are quite foolish and false. The ancient Jews were fighting for a way of life that set them apart. Their claim to morality was not inherent in their struggle, much less in their vulnerability, but in their acceptance of God's law and in their determination to obey it. They had to maintain this way of life, which was inherently Jewish, against all who would crush it, thereby crushing God's will. The suffering had no moral value in itself, but only as the required consequence of their moral way of life.

In the modern period, being singled out for mistreatment was something altogether different for Jews who no longer believed in their divine election or in Jewish religious observance. Could anti-Semitism be an occasion for improving the world if the Jews against whom it was directed no longer followed a strictly defined, God-inspired way of life? Two antithetical political ideologies said yes. One sought the enlistment of the Jew in a cause "higher" than his own, in a modern ideological system that went beyond the teachings of the rabbis; the other insisted on the Jew's own national legitimacy as part of the fabric of a modern pluralistic world community. Both movements held that the Jewish struggle, sublimated in the first instance, self-affirming in the second, could still be interpreted as an updated version of the biblical struggle of freedom versus oppression.

These alternatives did not prove equally benign. The sublimated striving for righteousness led straight to hell. True, there were Jewish idealists who under the socialist banner pioneered the trade unions and remained democrats. True, the motives of the Jewish internationalist socialists were usually pure, and their belief in the better-world-to-come often selfless and genuine. But the road to hell is paved with good intentions. The Jewish revolutionaries, Communists and pro-Communists, who justified expropriation, violence, and murder in the name of higher egalitarian ideals, should disabuse us once and for all of the notion that Jews are innately more moral than other people. The readiness of so many individual Jews to serve and to vindicate the most repressive political system in the world exposes the false claims of any "Jewish" morality apart from the morality of the Jewish Law. When it comes to Jewish enthusiasm for the great egalitarian project, I think we may be grateful that we are such a small people.

(One latest example of this phenomenon is the South African Nobel laureate for literature, Nadine Gordimer, born Jewish, who joined the African National Congress in spite of its justification of violence, its approval of Communism, and its ideological opposition to the Jewish state, and who enjoys moral credibility in many liberal Jewish circles for her "idealism." As has been the case throughout this century, when such Jews devote themselves to a movement that is not their own, their abandonment of the Jews is interpreted as transcendence of Jewish parochialism, and their abandonment of bourgeois morality is interpreted as proof of revolutionary commitment.)

By contrast with the blow that events have dealt these high-minded claims, the Jewish struggle for self-determination did remain an agent of liberalization, even within the revolutionary movement itself. When, for example, the members of the Jewish Socialist Bund insisted on their national legitimacy, they were resisting Lenin's concentration of power, whether or not that was their stated intention. This is why he opposed them so strenuously and had them crushed in the Socialist International. A similar demonstration of Jewish independence was manifested by the Soviet

Jewish refuseniks of the 1970s and 1980s. These Jews were called refuseniks because they were refused their request to emigrate to Israel, but their refusal was active, not passive. Like the gnat in talmudic legend that made its way into the brain of Titus and drove him insane with its buzzing, they refused to be intimidated in a system depending for its power on the ability to impose firm order on all. Jewish nationalism is a force for liberty because the will to be Jewish implicitly defies totalitarian hegemony. Since the Soviet Jew could hardly control the larger political forces, he could vouch for the morality of his cause only when he acted on his own behalf. Whatever its intentions, the universalist impulse contributed to the consolidation of totalitarian power, whereas the determination to remain Jewish at all costs kept alive the cause of liberty and justice.

Zionism was on even sounder moral ground than Bundism in its insistence on national self-determination—as long as it did not fall into the trap that Hess had unwittingly set for it, which was to combine the political ideal of a state with the secularized ideal of a holy nation. The fraudulence of Hess's original conception was exposed almost at once. Hess predicated his idea of a holy Jewish people on the model of the illustrious French! He wrote in 1862: "The Jewish nation . . . must not hesitate to follow France in all matters relating to the political and social regeneration of nations and especially in what concerns its own rebirth as a nation."

What a bitter joke on the idea of a national character! Some thirty years after Hess extolled the French spirit of *fraternité*, to him the essence of France's political identity, the Dreyfus case inspired Theodor Herzl to create a state to save the Jews from the French. France was the model, all right—the model of what would happen to the Jews if they remained dispersed throughout Europe in a period of emerging nation states. Hess certainly proved prescient in his generalization about the Germans as the most dangerous people in Europe, but before crediting his analysis of the character of nations it is worth remembering that his prophecies about the Teutonic national character were matched by correspondingly erroneous generalizations about the French.

Initially, of course, France had seemed also to the young Theodor Herzl the guarantor of European enlightenment and emancipation. Herzl (1860-1904) was raised in a liberal Jewish family in the Austro-Hungarian Empire, received his doctorate in law, and after making a name for himself in Vienna as a prolific journalist and writer, went to Paris as correspondent for the Vienna *Neue Freie Presse*, the most influential liberal newspaper of his day. In this way, he repeated the geographic trajectory of his precedessor, Moses Hess, and he, too, found in France his ideal of the modern state. He believed that by enfranchising the Jews, France had established an example of democracy, tolerance, and refuge from political oppression. When he became aware that social discrimination against Jews persisted, even in France, Herzl's first idea was that the Jews should completely assimilate themselves into French society, either through mass conversion in the Church or through the socialist movement.

Then came the Dreyfus case. In 1894 Captain Alfred Dreyfus was accused of passing military documents to the Germans, convicted of treason, and sent to Devil's Island.

A Light unto the Nations?

Anti-Semitism became manifest, not only in the trumped-up accusation that targeted Dreyfus because he was a Jew, but in the spontaneous Jew-hatred that erupted when Dreyfus was publicly humiliated. At the sight of the Paris mob shouting "Down with the Jews!" Herzl felt the collapse of his most cherished political assumptions. He would not have felt the humiliation so keenly had France not figured earlier as his promised land.

The crowd's hysteria threatened Herzl's deepest liberal faith. He wrote in his diary: "One Jew an alleged traitor and down with all the Jews? And where? In republican, modern, civilized France, 100 years after the Declaration of the Rights of Man!" Listen to his stunned disbelief. He was dazed not so much by the threat to the Jews as by the threat to himself, the civilized cosmopolitan, for whom the Declaration of the Rights of Man was the new Ten Commandments, the new Sermon on the Mount. Watching that frenzied anti-Semitic mob, he must have felt as Moses did when, coming down from the mountain with the perfect law for an exalted people, he found them dancing around a golden calf. When the shock began to wear off, Herzl went back up the mountain: Zionism was his revised attempt to rescue the liberal faith.

Because Herzl is the founder of the modern Jewish national movement, Jews inevitably parochialize his legend. Frightened they say, by the intensity of European anti-Semitism, Herzl determined to save his people from destruction. Herzl is regarded as the Jewish Galibaldi, champion of modern Jewish nationhood. This is true as far as it goes, but not true enough. Herzl's people were actually modern liberals among whom he was keen to include his own tribe, the Jews.

Zionism was the proposed solution not merely to the Jewish problem but to the European problem. If anti-Semitism could call into question the rational premises upon which French democracy rested, one would have to strengthen its rational premises by eliminating anti-Semitism. The depth of Jew-hatred released by the Dreyfus trial made Herzl realize that he could never resolve the disturbing exceptionalism of the Jews through assimilation, as he had originally thought. He would therefore have to quell the Jew-hatred through other means, by removing the object of French suspicion.

Moses Hess, troubled by the same problem, had blamed anti-Semitism on the German national character and found his solace in the higher national tolerance of the French. The Germans had made him see the need for a Jewish homeland; the French made it seem less urgent. For Herzl, who witnessed the moral collapse of France, no refuge was left. But no more than Hess was he prepared to surrender his optimistic belief in the perfectibility of human society through the rational acts of men and women.

This optimism was the source of what otherwise strikes us as Herzl's *chutzpah* or madness—his confidence that gentile rulers and assimilated Jews alike would come to his assistance. He trusted them to join him in the crusade to cure Europe of its hatred because he was convinced of the benefit that would accrue to all once the target of hatred was removed. Zionism was the last hope of European civilization, for unless Europe could find a rational and just solution to the Jewish problem, Europe itself could no longer pretend to be liberal, rational, or just. And it is true, of course, that had they been able to save themselves, the European Jews might have saved liberalism too.

Here, then, is the rub: Zionism was a movement not of pure but of tempered optimism. From its birth in troubled secular Europe, it required an acknowledgement of the destructive as well as the creative impulses of modern society, of the hateful forces that continued to retard the progress toward social improvement. Zionism required perhaps only temporary but still energetic and significant attentiveness to a small people whose fate exposed the depths of resistance to liberty, equality, fraternity. This is where it ran into trouble at the start, and where it flounders still. Those really infected by hatred cannot confront their own base prejudice, while those others who dream of a benign world order do not want to face the daily manifestation of malice and evil. Like Herzl before them, the defenders of the state of Israel today who insist on the rightful place of the Jews in the world are forced into perpetual confrontation with those who deny them that place. Jewish self-affirmation has never been an exercise for the weak, and in this respect, at least, the modern Jew who fights for Israel has something in common with his ancestor who broke from slavery to freedom.

Even posthumously—that is, not after Herzl's death but after the destruction of European Jewry—there are still liberals who resent the unwelcome realism that Jewish nationhood introduces into the modern world. Some object on philosophical or psychological grounds to admitting the fact of so much hatred, while others resent the effort required in standing up for the Jews. One might feel sorry for their timid souls, except that any pity wasted on them will result in the real death of Jewish children, sooner or later. Ironically, and contrary to so many professed good intentions, Jews do most to advance the liberal idea when they stand up to their enemies on their own behalf, and least when they assume excessive guilt in the hope of political absolution, or camouflage the defense of Jews as a loftier cosmopolitan cause.

One last point: how does this political struggle of Zionism to integrate the Jews into the family of nations square with the age-old Jewish claim to uniqueness? If Zionism demands no more than the normal existence of yet another country on the map, does this mean that Jews have to give up their moral striving to become a light unto the nations?

The contradiction is more apparent than real. Although the term "normalization" can point in two directions at once, there is no ambiguity in the Jewish demand for equal rights and equal treatment in the international arena. Normalizing the political status of the Jews as a modern nation depends exclusively and entirely on other nations; it could not in the past and cannot in the future be achieved without their cooperation. Israel has never been a normal country, because its Arab neighbours refused to accept the fact of its existence. Israel became the most abnormal country in the world when it alone was accused of racism for the crime of its existence. By defining Jews as the only contingent nation in the world, the Arabs kept alive their intention of destroying the Jewish homeland. Their political war against the Jewish state perpetuates in political terms the same conditional status that once defined the Jews under Christian and Muslim rule.

Political Zionism aimed for normalcy in this basic sense of

A Light unto the Nations?

unexceptionalism, a concept which puts the emphasis not on the adjustment of the Jews to the norms of other nations but on the adjustment of other nations to the normative existence of the Jews. In this, those international conventions of law and diplomacy that exist among nations were to apply equally to the Jewish nation, and any violation of those conventions was to be treated as an offense against the international order.

The emergence of nation-states in the nineteenth and twentieth centuries inspired the creation of a Jewish homeland. As we have seen, Moses Hess used the Italian risorgimento as the model for the consolidation of a modern Jewish state, and other examples might have served him just as well. But the urgency of the Jewish case was greater if Jews were to be rescued from surrounding nations, first in Europe, then in the Middle East, many of which defined their national aspirations as the right to expel, exclude, or exterminate the Jews. The Jewish state, in other words, was not only a normal modern political development but a response to the abnormal political passions in other countries. For the Jews to insist on their right to an unexceptional existence in the community of nations is therefore to discharge an obligation to the world as much as to themselves—at least if one wishes to continue believing in the world as a habitable human sphere. Faith in the family of nations is predicated on the world's ability to accept the political unexceptionalism of the Jews, who will have become a light unto the nations when they are no longer required as their scapegoat.

This aspiration for political unexceptionalism is entirely distinct from the impulse of conformism. Although many modern Jews of various political tendencies wanted to achieve "normalcy" in the sense of becoming more like everyone else, political Zionism did not imply Jewish conformity to the standards of other nations, because the very basis of the Zionist enterprise was to conserve and renew Jewish national distinctiveness, in one form or another. The substance of Jewish nationhood remains an entirely internal matter for the Jews and no one else to decide. Some nations have refined themselves, and others have befouled themselves, and it isn't at all clear from contemporary evidence which we ought to consider the norm.

The character of a nation is independent of its legitimacy, which is what Zionism sought first to guarantee. The scandal of Arab rejectionism almost half a century after the creation of the state of Israel is great enough. The scandal of Jews who overlook this outrage or accept it as a test of chosenness is an affront not only to Jewish life but to any moral life worth living.

Chapter Four

Tensions in the Family

Describing the family as the essential unit out of which all deeper attachments grow, Moses Hess alerts us in *Rome and Jerusalem* to both the resiliency of the Jewish nation as well as to the strains that have kept the Jews such a small people. The Jewish family used to be conceived—at least from the outside—as the very model of solidity, compensating through the cohesion of its membership for the punishing assaults that were launched against it. Experienced from the inside, however, its warmth may seem stifling. Philip Roth's fictional hero Alexander Portnoy complained that the *yid* was smothering the *id*. One of the most devoted and lifelong Zionists, Shemaryahu Levin (1867–1935), is said to have observed, "*Di yidn zaynen a kleyn folk, nor paskudne*" (Jews are a small people, but rotten). Such stinging judgments are better heard within the family than from a stranger's lips, but anyone who doesn't appreciate their wit has simply not spent enough time in the Jewish heartland. Whereas the forced intimacy of Jewish family and national life encourages a generous civilization of mutual responsibility, proximity also magnifies for one Jew the flaws of another.

First for the good news. In May 1991, the Israel Defense Forces in an operation spectacular even by their standards airlifted almost 15,000 endangered Ethiopian Jews to Israel despite the altogether predictable difficulties of integrating so large a group into a country already hard-pressed with obligations to the earlier wave of refugees from Russia. No other country on earth (with the possible exception of the United States) would have admitted, let alone sought out for rescue, people suffering from intestinal parasites, infants and aged people without means of support, a population that had not been introduced to cutlery and indoor plumbing, much less computer technology. If the nations of the world were capable of recognizing political truths, they might have seen that for the first time in history African blacks were being brought westward for purposes other than slavery. Far more than any of the theoretical foundations of modern Zionism, the idea of familial responsibility, now enshrined in national policy (and of which the Ethiopian airlift is but a small example), establishes Jewish practice in Israel.

In this respect of ingathering, there is a strong similarity between Israel and the United States: Each country was founded as a haven from persecution, and prides itself on the safety and freedom it guarantees to those denied it elsewhere.

Tensions in the Family

It seems fitting that the image of the Statue of Liberty, which was presented by the people of France to the people of the United States as testament to the common liberal hopes of both countries, should have been interpreted by the American Jewish poet Emma Lazarus as:

. . . .
Mother of Exiles. From her beacon-hand
Glows world-wide welcome; her mild eyes command
The air-bridged harbor that twin cities frame.
"Keep, ancient lands, your storied pomp!" cries she
With silent lips. "Give me your tired, your poor,
Your huddled masses yearning to breathe free,
The wretched refuse of your teeming shore.
Send these, the homeless, tempest-tost to me,
I lift my lamp beside the golden door!"

Emma Lazarus had watched the statue going up in New York harbor as she helped tend to the flood of Jewish refugees; to her, America was no extension of Europe but, for all those fleeing poverty and persecution, a welcoming *alternative* to Europe. (Palestine was another such place of refuge, and she was for the same reason a Zionist.) Her understanding of liberty was shaped by the biblical Exodus with its practical gloss on what liberty requires. Because America is free, she reasoned, it must open its door to unfortunates, and the opening of the door to unfortunates is what makes America free. As it happened, so true to the American spirit was

Lazarus's interpretation that her sonnet "The New Colossus," from which the above lines were taken, was affixed to the base of the statue in 1903, redefining the massive icon as a symbol of refuge. Certainly the American founding fathers were imbued with the cardinal biblical responsibility of being one's brother's keeper, and no one owes greater thanks to the haven they established than the Jews whom it rescued and (under certain Washington administrations more than others) continues to defend.

At first glance, the familial nature of Israel's ingathering appears to distinguish it from America's much more cosmopolitan hospitality. The Law of Return passed by the Israeli parliament in 1950 grants every Jew the right to enter the country not as an immigrant but as a citizen. Through this law, Israel tried to compensate the Jewish family that remained outside the borders of Israel for the historic losses and humiliations it had endured over the centuries by giving the Wandering Jew a home. If one traditional explanation for the expulsion of the Jews from their land was that God was punishing them for their sins, the state of Israel, like a kindlier, earthly father, declared itself the property of every Jew wanting to "return" to it. Ben Gurion made this explicit when he said that the state was not granting the right of settlement to Jews the way other countries—including Israel —sometimes grant entry to refugees; rather, the right of settlement belonged to every Jew simply by virtue of his being a Jew.

Some people consider this right to settlement overly exclusive. Since the development of modern secular democratic states is generally accepted as a significant advance over the older tribal forms of association, we are likely to take for granted America's moral superiority over Israel in making no legal distinction at the point of entry between the ethnicity and religion of one immigrant and another. In fact, Arab propaganda that attributes to the Jews its own intolerance accuses the Jews of racism for this unparalleled expression of fraternal responsibility. Yet were we to compare the immigration procedures of Israel and the United States by the standard of openness—in theory and in practice—the comparison would not necessarily work in America's favor. American immigration laws routinely limit the number and quality of refugees who may enter at any given time; whereas Israel's Law of Return declares that every Jew in the world has the right to settle in Israel as an *oleh*—an immigrant—at any time. The United States is so much more welcoming than most other countries that by comparison it looms as the most generous country in the world. But no matter how genuinely welcoming, American immigration policy is based on utilitarian considerations meant to benefit those who are already Americans. Israel, by contrast, admits all Jews irrespective of their personal assets. Non-Jews may not only apply to Israel for immigrant status on the same selective basis as to the United States and Canada, but more important, may elect to become Jews themselves. In this way, the Jewish state differs from all other national states, which have no such embracing possibility in their definitions of returning nationals. Whereas one can become an American—or a citizen of many another democratic country—only after being admitted into the country, implicit in the Jewish Law of Return is the ingathering of the entire human family since everyone who so desires can become a Jew. This openness of both the Jewish religion and the Jewish nation determines the character of the people and its political outlook. Israel's welcome of immigrants from Russia and Ethiopia is but the most recent demonstration of how the implicit idea of a particular nation expresses itself in political deeds.

Naturally, the influx of so many different kinds of Jews within a very short period of time into a very small and beleaguered country results in tension and strains, including complaints against the difficult new immigrants. It has become fashionable to portray Israel as a land torn apart by political discord. Reporters warn of an impending civil war between those who want to "return territories for peace" and those who "put their trust in power and land." In the case of some journalists, the conflict has been threatening for so long one suspects they can hardly wait for the first internecine murder to justify the note of panic they have been sounding year after year.

Divisions among the Jews in Israel are deep and real, yet not necessarily damaging in themselves. Just as the Renaissance and Reformation confirmed ruptures in the development of modern Christian societies, and just as the process of modernization reveals fissures inside the Arab world, so too, inevitably, Jewish society is divided in its attempt to adapt to accelerating technological change and over the direction such adaptations should take. Moreover, among Jews, debate is itself a major part of the tradition. Nowadays, within the same National Library in Jerusalem where modern scholars of comparative religion sit side by side with black-hatted yeshiva boys, the following sometimes occurs: the scholars who have

Tensions in the Family

come to understand the teachings after years of research, instruct the sectarian disciples in the meaning of the texts and are instructed in turn about practices and customs that only initiates could know. Elsewhere in the country, in cities and kibbutzim, are descendants of ardent Zionists and militant Communists, Jewish children raised to take pride in their national destiny and others taught to take pride in the dissolution of their national identity. The same familial intensity that produced the movement for Soviet Jewry and the Ethiopian airlift exacerbates the intensity of familial argument within a community that accepts debate as one of the identifying characteristics of the human animal.

Wars against the Jews have made the problem of national solidarity much more acute among them than among other peoples. The ceaseless aggression against them has had the contradictory effect of making Jews desperately dependent on one another and also resentful of that interdependence. In the 1930s and in the years preceding the establishment of Israel, civil discord among the Jews of Palestine, which would otherwise have figured as the healthiest sign of a democratic polity in the making, became a threat to national survival. Because no one has yet found a way of persuading most Arab rulers of Israel's permanent presence in the region, Israelis continue to argue among themselves the hypothetical question of what approach is likelier to overcome enemy resistance. The longer the argument continues, the stronger it grows. But so does the need for security.

The debaters know that unless their unity exceeds their fractiousness they will not see many new dawns. The continuing peril to their country seems to have forced Israelis into an uncommon and often unwelcome intimacy; deeply divided over how best to secure the peace, they nevertheless have no choice but to make common cause. Neighbors fight over whether Jews should settle in Arab-populated Hebron, then go off together on the evening civil patrol of the streets. An Israeli may become so angry at all major political parties that he threatens to emigrate—or to commit treason. Yet should you suggest to this man that his political disaffection may end by turning his children against their country, he bridles and informs you that one son is an officer with six years of military service, the other a candidate for the paratroopers, and his daughter a police sergeant. Even the Israeli who expresses his disagreement with others by going to war with himself, will join with others in the protection of his fellow Jews. This is the most significant difference between the Jews of Europe during the first half of the twentieth century and the Jews of Israel since 1948.

The demands of Israel on the individual Jew and citizen are greater than those in any other democracy, though Israelis will go to great lengths to deny it. A few years ago when I was in Tel Aviv attending a conference, my friends (whom I will call the Hofsteins) took me along to the ceremony marking their son's completion of basic training in the tank corps. Having seen photographs and newsreels of torchlight ceremonies against the bleak mountaintop of Masada, I thought I knew everything there was to know about this military rite of passage. Instead, I was surprised by everything I saw and heard, starting with the picnic basket Nina Hofstein packed for us and the mimeographed map she had received from the commanding officer to help parents find the way.

Tensions in the Family

The ceremony was held not at Masada but at Latrun, at the southern crossroads to Jerusalem. The army had decided it was too hard for families to make the trip down to a distant site in the desert and found a more convenient if less dramatic location between Tel Aviv and Jerusalem. Also, the government was eager to create a permanent memorial to the soldiers killed at Latrun in 1948, so it turned over the old police fortress there to the tank corps for a commemorative museum. The cars inching bumper to bumper along the dirt road and the parents noisily hunting down their children among the hundreds of soldiers, reminded me so much of my summers at camp in the Canadian Laurentians that I was hit by an incongruous wave of nostalgia.

The future tank brigade picnicked on the grass and amid the rocks until the sun began to set. To form the new museum, enemy tanks captured in each of Israel's wars had been brought to the site, and the younger Hofsteins had their fun scrambling over "Stalin II," a Russian-built trophy—if I can recall the summary details on the crude plaque—from the costly defense against Syria on the Golan Heights in 1967. The conversation at supper concerned baguettes: a determined new immigrant from France had discovered a way of turning Israeli flour and water into authentic French loaves. At one point the son we had come to fete told his parents he was to be cited as the top soldier of his unit, and the commanding officer wanted to congratulate them before the ceremony. Suddenly, everyone turned very shy. Afterwards, it seemed bad form to talk of the boy's distinction.

There was much in the program, as well as the natural setting, that reminded me of summer camp—the sloped seats of the makeshift amphitheatre, the eternal wait for the program to begin, and the strain of watching amateurs trying to act like professionals. What clinched the resemblance was the corps' entertainment troupe. In between speeches by the officers, the rabbi's invocation, and the presentation of arms, this musical ensemble of boys and girls offered a medley of songs; they sang of Shari's attraction to Ari the tank commander, of Micki's defection from Uri the mere infantry-man. I may not have the names exact.

It was hard to know what to make of this resolutely informal atmosphere. If no soldier's pledge to protect his country is ever taken lightly, Israel demands so much more from him over a lifetime as to have made the commitment different in kind. But rather than deliberately heightening the ceremonial aspect of soldiering—as I should have thought one must do when trying to convince a populace of its ultimate significance—the Israelis have altogether domes-ticated it. Except for the pledge itself, when I could feel the Hofsteins stiffening beside me, the whole evening was designed to be as casual as a local movie show.

The most familial note of all was struck by the commander who didn't look much older than his recruits. Here is what he said: "We in the corps know that you have entrusted to us your greatest treasures, your most prized possessions. Please be assured that your sons are our treasures too, and we know how to value them. We will care for them to the best of our ability. We will expose them to no needless danger. Even as we have to call on them to carry their part of the burden of security, we place a supreme worth on their lives, and their well-being." I almost expected him to spit three times as my mother does when she is trying to protect her children from the evil eye.

Hofstein, no fool, said to me following this little speech, "I hope no spy is present to tell our enemy how vulnerable we are." To which his wife Nina, referring to a recent prisoner exchange, snapped, "If we were prepared to release more than one thousand convicted Arab terrorists from our prisons in return for three Israeli soldiers, our enemies already know how vulnerable we are." But I sensed that neither parent was really unhappy to hear the young commander speaking so paternally of their children. He was only acknowledging what everyone in the country knows, that the division between soldiers and civilians is so fluid and reversible that no distinction can ever be made between defenders and sons.

So the customary emphasis in our media on Israel's political disunity is perversely misplaced. The story of the hour is not the split in the ranks of Israeli Jews but the continuing readiness of the large majority of Israelis to protect and mourn each other's children. Who, as late as the uprising in the Warsaw Ghetto, could have believed that any Jewish armed force would ever transcend party lines long enough to attack the enemy rather than a competing political faction? Certainly no one familiar with the lower depths of Jewish politics before the birth of the state.

The sustained importance of self-defense in the life of Israel sets it apart from all other democracies of the twentieth century and requires of every citizen an apprenticeship in arms that would elsewhere signify a commitment to military aggression. Only Switzerland among the other democratic countries of the world places an analogous burden of soldiering on its male population, though fortunately for the Swiss they have also their mountain ranges and their banking securities to help protect their independence. Yet there is no universal army service among Jews in Israel to correspond to their universal suffrage; the burden of defense does not fall equally on all alike.

In 1947, when David Ben-Gurion and the leadership of the Jewish Agency were claiming united Jewish support for the establishment of a Jewish state, they wanted to ensure that the anti-Zionist orthodox Agudat Israel would not breach the Jewish ranks. The so-called "status quo" agreement was then worked out, to confirm the privileged status within the about-to-be established state of the Sabbath, dietary laws, and matrimonial laws, and to offer guarantees of religious education. Though the negotiated settlement did not do much more than formalize certain practices that had been in effect under the British Mandatory government, its outcome set a pattern whereby the Orthodox minority was able to exploit critical moments of interparty strife to extend the religious boundaries of the "status quo." Exemption from military service for yeshiva students of Agudat Israel, which was part of the vague original agreement, involves no compensating national service of the kind other democracies require of their conscientious objectors. The handful of boys once affected by the arrangement has since grown more than a hundredfold.

One can readily sympathize with Ben-Gurion's predicament. Emotionally, he must have felt moved by this saintly remnant of a culture that had been so cruelly and unjustly erased, if not also a little guilty about his own part in having rebelled against it. Politically, he needed the broadest possible base of support, on his own behalf as the leader of a political party but also for the sake of a people that was facing serious external threats. But by introducing an exception into the requirements of citizenship, he destroyed the premise of equality upon which a democratic society rests. This separation of society, with one group assuming an obligation not binding on the other, would seem to contradict basic human standards of fairness and, by accepting the notion of a privileged spiritual elite, undermine the spiritual claims of the state itself. Tension between secular and religious impulses may not in themselves be a bad thing. Any democratic country can benefit from active competition between what are called "church" and "state," whatever the formal governmental relations between them. But exemption from national service in the name of the Lord, in a country that requires so much self-sacrifice from its citizens, corrupts the moral integrity of both religion and politics.

It must be stressed that this split in the Israeli population is not between secular and religious Jews, since some of the most dedicated recruits for the defense forces come from the ranks of modern orthodox yeshivas. While the kibbutz movement continues to set the standard for leadership in the armed forces, the Hesder yeshivas, which alternate rigorous study with periods of military service, are beginning to rival the kibbutzim in providing a new model of spiritually balanced soldiering. The division in the polity is rather between citizens who do and do not accept military service as a part of their obligations to it, who do and do not recognize the binding concept of citizenship.

The use of religion to lighten the load of citizenship is not a spiritual but a political maneuver that has cumulative political consequences. The ultraorthodox teachers insist that their students' long days of study are the supreme Jewish duty. But how do they deal with the masculine pride and fraternal conscience of these young men when all around them Jewish boys their own age sacrifice years of study, and much more, to protect them? The excused students must realize that only the national discipline of their fellow Jews ensures their religious freedom and their way of life. They must also know that they could not enjoy such cost-free bounty in any non-Jewish polity. The ideology that accepts all these benefits while scorning their source has to justify itself by ever more inflated spiritual claims.

I think of this whenever I read of black-hatted young men and boys with long earlocks throwing stones at offenders of the Days of Rest, or burning bus shelters featuring provocatively sexual ads, or when I overhear the quieter ones muttering *shabbes, shabbes* at transgressors of the Sabbath. In order to justify their abdication of national responsibility they have to be convinced that they too are really "soldiers" in a truer struggle, for how else could youngsters raised in the Jewish religious tradition accept the daily sacrifice of other Jews in their stead? When authority is invested in the people, as it is in a democratic country like Israel, defiance of authority is no longer an antidote to oppression as it was under csars and dictators, but a breach of the public trust. In the case of the twentieth-century Jews, who mobilized in effective self-defense only after one-third of their number had been destroyed, refusal to share in defense may be considered an act of aggression against one's own countrymen, one's children, and oneself. This is a serious perversion of a religion that places supreme value on individual life.

Conscription in Israel does not extend to Israeli Arabs. Although this exception, too, runs counter to the democratic idea of universality, here that principle is only temporarily violated. It is assumed that Arabs would not comfortably engage in battle against their fellow Arabs, at least not in alliance with Jews. If familial loyalty is to be credited as the model for mutual responsibility, members of a family should not be forced to go to war against one another in the name of any competing loyalty. Israeli Arabs are excused from military service as long as the Arabs are at war with Israel. The Rejectionist Front of Arab states (Syria, Iraq, Libya, South Yemen, Algeria, etc.), which coalesced in the 1970s to oppose any settlement with Israel, became even more militant after Egyptian President Sadat's peace initiative of November 1977. Were the Arab states that reject Israel finally to accept its presence within negotiated borders, the rights and responsibilities of Israeli Arabs would be adjusted accordingly—presumably along with the status of whatever Jews remain in Arab lands. Other non-Jewish non-Arab groups in Israel have been given the responsibilities they sought. The Muslim Circassians, for example, who came to Palestine from Russia over a century ago, demanded and were granted the right to serve in Israel's armed forces. So too the

Druze, at first only permitted to volunteer for service, had conscription imposed on them at their own request to put them on a par with Jewish citizens.

For obvious reasons, the Arabs within Israel proper, although citizens in all respects, have not yet followed suit. The full demands of their citizenship cannot be worked out until the larger Arab people of which they also form a part decides to coexist with another sovereign people in the Middle East. In the case of the ultra-Orthodox Jews, however, the issue of civic equality can hardly be postponed, because it is not contingent on external political change and because it runs counter to both familial and civic notions of equity.

What about the Jews of the Diaspora and their share of responsibility for Israel's defense? And what about the question of dual loyalty, which is raised about Jews who assume responsibility for Israel's defense? The vulnerability of the Jewish people does indeed confront them with a unique dilemma, though not with the choice of loyalties as it is generally described.

Israel's Law of Return, entitling all Jews to claim the country as their own, means that no Jew will ever again want for a place of refuge. Naturally, like any other law, it is not without its problems of interpretation. Is a convicted Jewish criminal to be given asylum as a Jew, or treated according to the laws of *his* country? Does the law apply to apostates who claim that they are ethnic Jews despite their religious conversion? Thorniest of all is the question implicit in the Law of Return, namely, who is a Jew? When some Orthodox Israeli politicians recently tried to clarify the Law of Return as it pertains to converts by limiting it to those who follow the Orthodox process of conversion, they raised the ire of the Reform and Conservative movements of America. The ensuing confrontation between representatives of Diaspora Jewry and Israeli officialdom were exceptionally spirited, reflecting passionate fraternal possessiveness on the part of Jews outside Israel for what is also *their* homeland.

Yet brotherhood is complicated by the fact that its claims are, or could become, reciprocal. The haven of Jews is also theirs to protect, and the Law of Return, which enunciates the responsibility assumed by Israeli Jews for those outside the country, can also be read as a statement of mutual obligation. Diaspora Jews were right to protest artificial attempts to define them (though some arguments of the Conservative and Reform movements were not necessarily persuasive), since they cannot leave it to a section of the Israeli rabbinate to determine who they are and what makes them Jews. If Israel were in trouble, however, would these Jews be required to protect it to the same degree as its own Jewish citizens? Is the law equally binding on both partners?

Hillel Halkin, an American Jew who settled in Israel, argues that the Jewish state, once established, became the only place for a Jew to live. His Zionist polemic, *Letters to an American Jewish Friend,* published in 1977, is addressed to an American Jew like himself who despite warm feelings for Israel and commitment to Jewishness is quite content to remain in the United States. The American friend resents the guilt that Israelis made him feel in the early days of statehood and expresses satisfaction that during an entire summer in Israel no one had asked him the dreaded question,

"When are you coming here to settle?" But Halkin is disturbed by the Israeli reticence, arguing:

> Because there is, or at least, should be, an unavoidable tension in the relationship between an Israeli and a Diaspora Jew, a relationship which is ideally an adversary one since the Israeli is living in a community of faith which holds that it alone is the natural place for a Jew to live, and this tension can only be resolved by dealing with it directly. A Diaspora Jew and an Israeli can talk to each other as ordinary human beings about anything they wish—about the Palestinian question, or the high price of air travel, or the last words of Heidegger, or even the poetry of Yehuda Halevi—but if they are to talk to each other meaningfully as Jews, there is, alas, only one relevant question with which such a conversation can begin, which is one that no one asked you this summer.

This version of the Zionist faith makes the ingathering of all Jews into Zion an obligation rather than an opportunity, and considers the Law of Return to be a constantly beckoning duty. Halkin argues through the logic of numbers: He threatens the Diaspora with demographic omens of disappearance to underscore the exigency of immigration. Another such Zionist, the Israeli novelist Amos Oz, argues that creative vitality is possible only in Israel. He contrasts Jewish national creativity inside Israel with the absence of such creativity elsewhere, calling Israel the theater of action, the Diaspora merely its audience.

Hillel Halkin's polemic and the imagery of Amos Oz are admirably passionate, but neither on its theoretical nor its practical merits can *aliyah*—immigration of the Jews to Israel—be accepted as dogma. For one thing, the story of the

Israelites as recorded in the Bible includes the lengthy sojourn of at least part of the people in Egypt. Although the Bible certainly does not glorify this chapter of Jewish history, neither does it deny the persistence of Jewish life outside the land of Israel for hundreds of years at a time. More to the point, after so many centuries on other continents, a people as adaptive as the Jews cannot suddenly be made to believe that its creative survival will depend on geography alone. North Americans in particular could never be convinced by an article of faith that is contradicted by their personal experience. Long before the modern Jewish state came into being, the United States Constitution (and, almost to the same degree, the British North America Act governing Canada) promised a home to people of all faiths and nationalities, and the millions of Jews born into these freedoms since then cannot deny their roots in America or their love for their country. If Israel is unquestionably the Jewish homeland, America is just as surely a homeland of the Jews—no less than of the resident English, Italians, Irish, Dutch, Africans, or Japanese.

It complicates Zionism to have succeeded in rebuilding the Jewish state only after one-third of the Jews had been killed and another third had found a trusted home. But of the two complications, only the first was fatal. No people with a will to live ever perished through surfeit of opportunity.

Halkin is right about the unavoidable tension in the relationship between an Israeli and a Diaspora Jew who are determined to be honest with each other. But the source of the tension is less metaphysical or ideological than practical. Israel is the only modern country still rejected by all but one of its neighbors after five major wars and almost fifty years. One group of Jews bears the brunt of this anti-Jewish assault; the other does not. Some day, when the Jewish homeland is as unthreatened as, say, Canada, the presence of an individual Jew here or there would matter no more than does the presence or absence of any average Canadian in Canada. Until that time, Jewish bodies have to be counted, and the Law of Return can be read as a summons.

In saying this, I don't mean to trivialize the large questions of Jewish destiny or the Jewish people. Yet the problems of a political state are finite, and separate from the familial trauma of its inhabitants. The guilt incurred by the Israeli who leaves his country today is not a function of his Jewishness or even of his Zionism but of the siege that encircles his fellow citizens. His departure increases, psychologically and numerically, their burden of defense.

During the Yom Kippur War of 1973, one of my colleagues at McGill flew back to join his combat unit. He sent us a postcard signed, "The Fist of the Jewish People." Afterward he apologized for the melodrama and the innuendo of resentment, but the resentment was honest. For most of the time he was among us we spoke, like the people in Halkin's description, about Samuel Beckett and the structure of biblical narrative. And why not, since these were our common concerns as teachers of literature? But at the moment of assault, everything that had been left unsaid between us crystallized into the plain fact that while we in Montreal would continue to talk about Beckett and the Bible, he would be dragging his unwilling—and already battle-damaged—body back into the ugliest of human activities. It makes you wonder whether the perpetual talk in the multiplying institutes and centers for Israel–Diaspora dialogue isn't meant to obscure the question Halkin rightly says we ought to be asking: Who is going to Israel to settle?

Does this then mean that diaspora Jews are less trustworthy citizens of their own countries because they owe allegiance to the Jewish people? Does the Law of Return, by offering Jews a homeland, provoke their disloyalty to other countries? We will return to the question of Jewish loyalty in a later chapter, but perhaps it can be anticipated here with a quotation from a naive source, the posthumously discovered *Diary* of Anne Frank. The exceptionally long diary entry for 11 April 1944 records the events of the preceding weekend when an attempted burglary in the building almost resulted in the discovery of the families who lived there in hiding, and probably did trigger off a chain of inquiry that culminated in their arrest by the Gestapo three months later. Anne's tension explodes in an extended exclamation:

Who has inflicted this upon us? Who has made us Jews different from other people? Who has allowed us to suffer so terribly up till now? It is God that has made us as we are, but it will be God, too, who will raise us up again. If we bear all this suffering and if there are still Jews left when it is over, then Jews, instead of being doomed, will be held up as an example. Who knows, it might even be our religion from which the world and all peoples learn good, and for that reason and that reason only do we have to suffer now. We can never become just Netherlanders, or just English, or representatives of any country for that matter, we will always remain Jews, but we want to, too.

Be brave! Let us remain aware of our task and not grumble, a solution will come, God has never deserted our people. Right through the ages there have been Jews, through all the ages they have had to suffer, but it has made them strong too; the weak fall, but the strong will remain and never go under!

During the night I really felt that I had to die, I waited for the police, I was prepared, as the soldier is on the battlefield. I was eager to lay down my life for the country, but now, now I've been saved again, now my first wish after the war is that I may become Dutch! I love the Dutch, I love this country, I love the language and want to work here. And even if I have to write to the Queen myself, I will not give up until I have reached my goal.

Anne's spirit is robust and resilient. First she finds some reassurance for herself as a Jew, and in the next breath, she declares her passionate love of the Netherlands. Her loyalty to the Jews releases her loyalty to the Dutch in a way that is thoroughly characteristic of most modern Jews, who bring to their countries of residence and citizenship a heightened, magnified, gratitude for being allowed to live there in peace. Anne Frank's love for the Dutch is not in conflict with, but the corollary of her need for comfort as a Jew. Jewish loyalty has always, and particularly in the modern period, begotten a *doubled* loyalty to those who accept them. Jews become turncoats only in the face of anti-Jewishness, and then, as we shall see, they usually turn against their fellow Jews.

The Jews of today could be likened to a family some of whose children stay home to care for mother and father while others go off on their own. (Some might want to represent a country as young as Israel as the common child of the Jewish people, which would increase the obligation to care for it.) As long as the parents are healthy, the children at a distance can discharge their share of responsibility by sending money as it is needed and by coming often to visit. Their absence does not deprive their parents of them to any greater degree than it deprives them of their parents.

But if the parents are plagued by illness the balance of family life changes. Those at home are forever on guard. They spend days at the doctor's, in the hospital, at a bedside. All their plans for tomorrow and next week are nervous and contingent. The interruptions to their work and love affairs and thoughts are bound to stir resentment, the longing to be released. Even when the ailing parents enjoy a few good days in succession, the relief is only temporary.

What of those at a distance? Their sympathetic letters are accompanied by larger sums of money to help defray the mounting costs of nursing care. On their visits they may even express regret and remorse at being so far from the heart of the family. But given the choice, they would prefer to stay away and let other members of the family continue to perform the required duties.

The Jewish mother-and-fatherland suffers from a new strain of an affliction that has destroyed too many Jewish communities in the past. We all dream of a cure or, short of that, of long periods of remission. In the meantime, however, those in Israel and those not in Israel know which of them carries the heavier share of the filial burden, and nothing Jews say to one another across the oceans can mitigate that knowledge.

Chapter Five

The Demonization of Israel

During our lifetime, as ideological anti-Semitism went into brief remission, Jews enjoyed what might be called a quarter-century of grace. Between the establishment of Israel in 1948 and the introduction of the Zionist-Racist equation at the United Nations in 1975, Jews seemed poised to win the acceptance they had been seeking in the international community. As long as the memory of Auschwitz-Birkenau was fresh and while Arabs still cast themselves as belligerents in the wars against the infant state, Jews figured as unquestionable victims and underdogs, hence as a respectable liberal cause. You could not tell a people that had so recently been pushed into the ovens that you were going to "push them into the sea" without stiffening national resolve and without stirring the conscience of the West. In those years, the West

117

could better afford its conscience: Oil was not yet the controlling weapon it became in the 1970s, and Israel was sparing the world a headache by absorbing the neediest and most damaged refugees, including almost a million Jewish refugees from Arab countries. Political grace is the prerogative not of God, but of governments that tolerate the Jews and accept them at par with other groups. The years 1948–1975 formed a period of grace because for the first and only time in this century, despite military aggression against Israel, no state-supported ideology of anti-Semitism was being disseminated to render the Jews exceptional and exceptionable.

In America, these were years of unprecedented self-confidence. Untouched by the Holocaust and unburdened by the rigors of securing Israel, American Jews benefited equally from sympathy for the annihilated European victims and admiration for the gritty Israeli underdogs. Discrimination against Jews abated to the point that "identity" became the main concern. Since the retention of their ethnic distinctiveness is more voluntary among Jews than among minorities of distinctive race or color, Jews felt themselves under increasing pressure to secure from within the boundaries between themselves and their fellow-Americans that had previously been reinforced from without.

The period of grace ended when the Arab nations resuscitated ideological anti-Semitism, holding Jews responsible for the crime they intended to commit against them. Anti-Israel politics had been the strongest unifying force of the Arab world for decades, but the military defeats that the Arabs suffered in 1967 and again in 1973 in their collective efforts to destroy Israel had the paradoxical effect of opening up an entirely new front in their war. It allowed the Arabs to accuse Israel of aggression for the crime of having successfully defended its territory and on the fertile ground of anti-Jewish prejudice, in the language already fashioned by Communism in the 1930s, to flesh out once again the myth of a Palestinian Arab liberation movement that was struggling against an outpost of Western imperialism.

The ideological attack on Israel as the illegitimate occupier of Arab land was as blatantly unprovoked and unjust as the military confrontations that preceded it. Every country, emphatically including every one of the many Arab countries, can be said to exist at the expense of another. Arabs, having conquered more civilizations than any other people in history, are in the weakest position of all to deny the rights of conquest to a single, tiny Jewish state. Indeed, Jews have more concurrent rights to their land than any other people on this earth can claim: aboriginal rights, divine rights, legal rights, internationally granted rights, pioneering rights, and the rights of that perennial arbiter, war. The target of the Palestine Liberation Organization, established when Jordan and Egypt still controlled the West Bank and Gaza, was, incontrovertibly, Israel, which it aimed to "liberate" from the Jews. Arab rejectionism always disclaimed the existence, not the dimensions of the Jewish state.

If Palestinian Arabs became permanent refugees (while Jewish refugees from Arab countries were reabsorbed as new Israeli citizens), it was because Arab governments did not allow the partition of Palestine in the first place, nor resettlement of Arab refugees thereafter. Until 1967 the Arabs, being in possession of the West Bank and Gaza, could have fashioned for their brothers and sisters a separate state, or quickly resettled them within the already predominantly Palestinian state of Jordan, or made some other provisions for their political autonomy within a greater Jordan. A few minutes in any local library is enough to ascertain that Jordan—even after the partition in 1948 and the loss of the West Bank in 1967—still occupies 78 percent of the territory of Palestine, all of which was actually promised to the Jewish national home in 1920. Regarding Israel's claim to the disputed territories, Eugene V. Rostow, former U.S. under secretary of state and expert in international law, writes:

> Israel is occupying the administered areas not only as the victor in the defensive wars of 1967 and 1973, and as a claimant to the territory, but pursuant to a legally binding decision of the Security Council of the United Nations— that is, a decision by the unanimous vote of the Great Powers and of the rotating members of the Council. That legally binding decision, embodied in Security Council Resolutions 242 and 338, ratifies a package deal made in 1967 after the Six-Day War, that Israel should remain in occupation of these territories until the states of the area make a just and lasting peace with Israel, as Egypt did [in 1979]. That peace, the Security Council ruled, should rest on two principles—Israeli withdrawal from some but not necessarily all the territories occupied during the Six-Day War, on the one hand, and recognition by the Arab states of Israel's right to live in peace within secure and recognized boundaries, free from threats or acts of force. Anatoly Dobrynin, the Soviet ambassador in Washington at the time, said that Resolution 242 was the only occasion during

The Demonization of Israel

the history of the Cold War that the Soviet Union used the phrase "package deal" in a positive sense.

Rostow explains why the question of Israel's presence in the administered territories had to be linked to Arab acceptance of Israel's presence, as if something as elementary as the need for Arab recognition should have required explanation. Israel was never in the past and in the future will never be able to "settle" Palestinian Arabs successfully or to accommodate them politically without first being guaranteed unconditionally its own right to flourish. Meanwhile, Palestinian Arabs are the only refugees in the world to have been armed and paid and forced by their Arab brothers to *resist* the political accommodation they were offered.

But as already shown, facts are irrelevant to political anti-Semitism, which operates through a logical consistency of its own. The Big Lie is the attribution to the target of one's aggressive intentions against it. Untrue by definition, it compensates through the vigor of prosecution for the irrationality of its claims. Arab leaders had no trouble charging the Jews with racism; they were convinced that the Middle East belonged exclusively to them and that anyone denying their hegemony was racist.

Arabs object to being compared to the Germans and justifiably, because in all respects but one they are as different from one another as peoples can be—different as the Middle East is from Central Europe, Islam from Christianity, sun-dried sands from rain-soaked forests. The contrast between them, however, makes the single point of identification all the more startling, since the organization of Arab national-

ism around the negative image of the Jew owes everything to
the German precedent, and even takes Nazi ideology one
step farther. The Zionism-equals-racism inversion works
exactly like the Nazi accusations against Jewish world conspirators, the aspiring expansionists attributing to the Jews
their own aim of conquest and their own racist intolerance
for another national–religious group. But while European
anti-Semitism wanted to "solve the Jewish problem" by
eliminating or destroying the Jews of Europe, Arab anti-
Zionism wants to displace the Jews by replacing them with
another Arab people.

Why else have Palestinian Arabs shaped their national
identity almost exclusively through usurped Jewish symbols
and history? They say they are the Arab diaspora, longing for
their homeland. The PLO writes a "covenant," a sacred
document like the one in the Torah, that promises the land of
Israel to them, the Arabs. They launch a ship called the
Exodus to draw attention to Arab plight. They claim to be
suffering a Holocaust at the hands of the Jews. They initiate
the United Palestine Appeal, with the map of Israel as its
logo. A spokeswoman of the Palestinian Arabs, widely
perceived as a new model of moderation, holds up the picture
of a dead Arab girl as the Palestinian "Anne Frank." The
systematic appropriation by Arabs of Jewish symbols robs Jews
of their national dignity and puts them on notice that
another people intends to replace them. Still more frightening is what this habit of inversion tells us about the nature of
Palestinian identity. For if the Palestinian Arabs consider
themselves a nation, how and why do they represent themselves consistently as Jews? It seems hard to resist the

conclusion that replacement of the Jews is the cornerstone of Palestinian nationalism.

Of the sheer propaganda success of this strategy of inversion there can be no doubt. When an American Arab, returning to his "picturesque Arab village," is quoted by the *New York Times* as having told his friends with pride, "It's changing, we're being seen more as victims than as terrorists," both the pride and the claim to victimization testify to a changed image not just of the Palestinian Arabs but of Israel—a change that the *Times* has itself done much to promote. The attack on the moral standing of the Jewish state accomplished what military warfare alone could never have achieved. It made people, including many Jews both in the diaspora and in Israel itself, question the moral worth of Israel, and thereby begin to rationalize the Arab aim of destroying it. Although the resolution equating Zionism and racism was finally repealed by the United Nations, the concept was simultaneously reaffirmed at the Muslim summit in Dakar in December 1991. In other words, the Arab countries still feel justified in trying to destroy Israel, and intend to continue their campaign of vilification against it. What is America likely to do about this assault in the years ahead?

Political debate in democracies is broadly divided into Right and Left, conservative and liberal, Republican and Democrat. The advancement of social programs, economic measures, legislative changes, and foreign policy decisions depends on the support of at least one of these two sides of the political spectrum and ideally of both, each for its own reason. But the support of Israel against much stronger enemies, like the support of the Jewish minorities while they were still dispersed among the nations, puts a severe strain on both sides of the political balance. Through moral inversion and moral equivalence—blaming the Jews wholly or in part for the aggression aimed against them—both conservatives and liberals may abandon Israel without unnecessary pangs of conscience.

The view from the Right looks as follows: the asymmetry between about 13 million Jews and Israelis on one hand and a coalition of almost 1 billion Muslims and Arabs on the other dominates any assessment of their relative value as allies. Normally, a neutral country need not necessarily favor either of two warring sides and can try to cultivate trading relations with both. But the Arab war against Israel is not a normal conflict. Arab refusal to recognize the existence of Israel, buttressed by the longest economic boycott in modern history, forces other countries to choose between them, a choice democratic countries eventually come to resent because of the restrictions it places upon them. Since self-interest favors the Arab, it is altogether predictable that the resentment of the Right will mount against the Jew.

During the years of the Cold War, Israel provided the United States with a clear advantage in the Middle East. Because Israel had to defend itself against Arab attackers who were backed, in turn, by Soviet arms, Soviet aid, and Soviet intelligence, the country became a military outpost of great strategic importance in the defense against Communism. The decision of once unfriendly Republicans like Jesse Helms to lend Israel political support may be credited to this perceived benefit from Israel's trustiness as an ally in an area of otherwise undemocratic and notoriously unreliable political states. But Israel's bargaining powers have always been limited. Its dependability may be construed as merely a function of its dependence on the United States and hence discounted in advance. The accelerating turn of American foreign policy against Israel under the Bush administration from the minute that the Soviet Union began to unravel in earnest demonstrates how little hard political power Israel wields when the United States is without a military challenger, or thinks it has found alternative allies among the Arabs.

An early portent of conservative accommodation to Arab politics in democratic countries was the description, in November 1967 by President Charles de Gaulle of France, of the Jews as an elite and domineering people and of the Six-Day War as a pretext for Israel "to grab the objectives it wished to attain." Up to the mid-1960s, France supported Israel and was one of its chief suppliers of arms. Then, in the aftermath of the Algerian war, in which France had appeared to be pitted against the Arab world, President de Gaulle saw a chance to reestablish his country's influence in a region where neither the Soviet Union nor the United States was wholly trusted. France's heavy dependence on Arab oil added urgency to this political ambition. The fastest and simplest way to appeal to the Arabs was through the political shorthand of turning against the Jews.

Blaming Israel and the Jews made it possible for this former hero of the French anti-Nazi resistance to pursue mercenary policies with an air of righteousness and self-congratulation. In the words of one observer, "de Gaulle needed an opportunity to distance himself from Israel in a manner that could dramatically project him as an ally of the Arab cause, while protecting him from the reaction of pro-Israel public opinion" in his own country. De Gaulle's moral repudiation of Israel camouflaged France's political abandonment of Israel and its capitulation to Arab might. The country's foremost Jewish intellectual, Raymond Aron, said, "the anti-Semites had received solemn authorization from the Head of State to make themselves heard again and to employ the same language as before the Final Solution."

Let me offer a more recent example from my own country, Canada. On March 10, 1988, invited by the Canada-Israel Committee to address its annual conference, Minister of External Affairs Joe Clark of the ruling Conservative party used the occasion to charge Israel with using unnecessary brutality to quell the Intifada, the violent uprising of Palestinian Arabs that had begun the previous year. He also accused Israel of trying to starve Palestinian Arabs by holding back convoys of food, an accusation as fabricated as it was malicious. This was surely the first time in Canadian history that a politician had used the gathering of an ethnic or religious group to defame a constituency that had come seeking traditional reassurances, and no politician in a democratic country would have done such a thing had the political prize not justified the political risk. But Clark was not talking to the Jews. In return for this hard-line, widely reported anti-Israel speech, Canada received the support of all the Arab countries in its bid for a seat on the Security Council, one of the longstanding priorities of Canadian External Affairs. From the government's point of view, blaming Israel had the double advantage of winning Arab

The Demonization of Israel

political support—far beyond this single issue—and of absolving the government for its failure to protect Israel against its Arab enemies.

Every democracy wants to pursue its legitimate interests in the Middle East, which means courting Arab markets, bargaining for Arab oil, and seeking political alliances with Arab powers. As long as Arab governments require that the democracies tilt against Israel as a condition for maintaining relations, they exact a moral price for their favors. Given incentives of such a scale, the Arab distortion begins to flow into the stream of Western political consciousness as readily as Arab oil flows into Western refineries. By blaming Israel for its own predicament, or by attacking Israel for abusing the rights of others, politicians and large parts of their constituencies can satisfy both their consciences and their interests and pretend that the two are one.

The view from the Left is progressively shaped by the Arab war of ideas against Israel, which—unlike the failed military attempts to destroy the country—enjoys remarkable success. The most obvious explanation for this success lies in the strength of its human and financial resources. Tens of millions of dollars have been paid by Arab propagandists on this continent to groups and individuals for their work in defaming Israel. Since this is not an advertising campaign working in the open, neither the size of its budget nor the nature of its operation is ever made public, and it is hard to differentiate between its paid executives and volunteers. We may recall that the word "propaganda" originated with a committee of cardinals of the Roman Catholic Church who sought to propagate the Faith in foreign lands, and that the most effective disseminators of any doctrine have always been its true believers. Without question, the Palestinian Arabs and others who go abroad to preach against Israel are convinced of the justice of their mission, and their single-minded conviction that Jews have usurped their lands is sufficient proof to many listeners of the justice of what they seek. True faith is infectious, and advertising pays—hate advertising like any other.

The visibility and volubility of Arab protest against Israel's treatment of the Palestinian Arabs stands in such glaring contrast to Arab silence on other much more serious issues such as the slaughter of the Kurds in Iraq and of the Muslims in Hama, Syria, that one is bound to see the connection between promotion of one and suppression of the other. There are, of course, a great many Arabs and Muslims who privately share the democratic aspirations of their fellow citizens, but there does not seem to be much more than a single Fouad Ajami bold enough to call for self-criticism and self-scrutiny as the cornerstone of an Arab liberalism. Thus, while Arab activists look for any occasion of Jewish self-affirmation, such as a Judaica library exhibit or a luncheon for Israel Bonds, to mount protests against Jewish "racism," they as scrupulously refrain from protesting even the most glaring abuses of personal freedom and human rights in their own countries and in other Arab countries of the Middle East.

Incredibly, as far as I can determine, no attempt has ever been made, either on the part of a United States governmental agency, or on the part of the B'nai B'rith Anti-

Defamation League, to chart and estimate the cost of the
Arab propaganda war waged on the North American continent and everywhere in the world against Israel and the Jews.
Only through such an investigation could we assess the
cost-effectiveness of the campaign to turn public opinion
against Israel, through the United Nations and its agencies,
through oil companies, the business community, and the
unions, and in the supremely sensitive area of education at
the elementary, high school, and university levels. In its
inventory of armaments, *Jane's* does not monitor propaganda
expenditures and resources as it does military budgets and
hardware; yet the destruction of the image of the Jews has
always been the necessary precondition for physical attacks
upon them.

Resources of money are matched by resources of intellect.
Although a single example cannot do justice to the expand-
ing range and increasing refinement of anti-Israel materials,
the analysis of one such document may demonstrate the
sophisticated nature of Arab propaganda in English targeted
to North American audiences. The following advertisement
for the "United Palestine Appeal" ran in 1991 during the
Gulf War, under the headline, "Palestinian Children Need
Not Suffer in Silence." A little girl sits hunched in a
wheelchair, looking miserable and crushed, beside a quotation attributed to Marc H. Ellis, Maryknoll School of
Theology, New York: "In Jerusalem, in Nablus, in Ramallah
and in the Gaza. The soldiers guard the return against the
enemy. . . . Hospitals full of children beaten, shot paralyzed,
brain dead." The elliptical style is typical of a cast of mind

that does not require evidence because it demonizes the Jews as the wanton killers of innocent Arab children. The rest of the text is as follows:

> Lulu, a 7-year-old girl from Rafah refugee camp in Gaza Strip, enjoyed a normal life until she was shot in the head by Israeli troops while returning from school. She is now paralyzed and unable to speak.

> Lulu is only one example of thousands of Palestinian children killed, injured or left homeless during the Intifada.

> While the world's attention is focused on the Gulf crisis, the killing of Palestinian children under 15 in the Occupied Territories continues.

> 217 children killed. Over 50,000 children injured. In U.S. population terms, these casualties represent: 13,200 American children dead. 3,380,000 American children injured.

> These punishing collective measures will have a lasting psychological effect on Palestinian children. They urgently need proper health care, rehabilitation, shelter, education and security. UPA is a non-political, non-profit charity that works with local organizations in the Occupied Territories to provide essential services for Intifada victims.

> With your support, many of these victims may again live normal lives.

Tax-deductible contributions are directed to the appropriate address and bank.

The *United Palestine Appeal* is a deliberate parody of the United Israel Appeal, the chief arm of Jewish philanthropy since the creation of the state, before which *it* was called the

United Palestine Appeal. This inverted terminology is a double act of usurpation, first in replacing the existing state of Israel by an Arab state that will erase it, second, in stealing the vocabulary of diaspora Jews to turn it against them. In some of its material the United Palestine Appeal carries the logo of the map of Israel, graphically representing the intention of taking over what the Jews have wrought.

How can we be certain that this is a mock organization, rather than a real attempt to assist suffering Arab children? The original United Palestine–United Israel Appeal maintains the tradition of communal self-help that has always characterized the Jews as a people. Through a network of volunteers wherever there is a sizeable Jewish population, it uses social incentives and (because there is no tithing) social pressure to raise the monies necessary for the resettlement of Jewish refugees in Israel, and for local communal needs. Arab resources, alas, are directed toward exactly the opposite end. The United Palestine Appeal does not collect money from Arabs for the assistance of suffering Arab children through any philanthropic infrastructure in Arab overseas communities, nor have wealthy Arabs established philanthropic institutions analogous to those of the Jews. Had the education and welfare of Palestinian Arab children been a goal of Arab charity, the Arabs would by now have funded hundreds of organizations like those of the Alliance Israelite, the Joint Distribution Committee, the Organization for Rehabilitation through Training, Hadassah-WIZO and Youth Aliyah, Pioneer Women (whose origins was in Zionist socialism), Emunah (whose membership is traditional orthodox), and so forth. Wealthy Arabs all over the world would be supporting in Hebron, Gaza, as well as Amman, a full network of Israeli-style universities and institutes, music schools, sports facilities, religious academies, schools for the handicapped, financed largely by overseas monies. Jews did not consider political advantage the prerequisite for helping one another; many of the existing Jewish charities were established throughout the diaspora independently of Zionist ideals, because the education and health of Jewish children in Morocco and Poland as well as in Palestine was a sufficient end in itself.

Thus, the mock Palestinian appeal is only a weapon to destroy the moral image of the Jews. When addressing their own people in Arabic, Arabs are not embarrassed to appeal directly to Arab values, primary among them the conquest of land. Out in the liberal West, however, they adopt the local language of ideas, translating aggression into the vocabulary of a different culture. Lulu is being used in the advertisement as an instrument of anti-Israel propaganda rather than as part of a bona fide appeal for aid to children, by the same logic that the Palestine Liberation Organization places its arsenal in schools and shelters using the bodies of Arab children as political weapons and shields. The double inversion of Arab hatred into a Jewish-style concern for child welfare and of the Israelis as Arab-style killers is, on its merits as political warfare, worthy of admiration.

Propaganda this clever is very hard to defend against, for who would presume to deny an appeal on behalf of a wounded little girl, or dare to object to the impulses of sympathy that are elicited by her abject misery? Through layout, diction, and imagery, aggression against the Jews is so successfully transformed into compassion for the Arabs that one can hardly identify the murderous impulse beneath the protestations of concern.

In general, Arab opposition to Israel made remarkable gains when in the 1970's it exchanged the language of the Right for the language of the Left, presenting Israel as the bloodthirsty exploiter of impoverished innocent Arab masses. For its part, the Soviet Union was delighted to help promote anti-Zionism as the unifying political bond of an Arab-Communist bloc, just as it had done in 1929. At that time, following the Arab uprising in Palestine, the ruling Comintern pronounced the massacres of the Jews in Safed and Hebron the beginning of a popular Arab uprising against British and Zionist imperialism, and directed leftist sympathies to the Arab perpetrators of the pogroms. All the recent slogans of Arab propaganda—including the equation of Zionism with racism, the promotion of Arabs as the revolutionary proto-proletariat, and the cultivation of such Arab symbols as Lulu—derive from the Communist press of those years. The Soviets had only adopted the Arab cause in a cynical attempt to enlarge their sphere of influence, but the adoption of leftist terminology did more for the Arab cause than the Communists ever intended. As the Right turns against Israel to camouflage its material self-interest, so the Left turns against Israel to protect its ideological self-interest. In this, both the Left and the Right are repeating the patterns of the first half of this century.

The propaganda of inversion has a guaranteed advantage over the military effort to destroy Israel: it meets with no resistance. Every educated person believes that he is immune to propaganda, but if he could fairly imagine the Pepsi "challenge" without a response from Coca-Cola, he might begin to appreciate the cumulative effect of a negative information campaign. When Pepsi-Cola tried to boost its sales by explicitly proving its superiority to Coca-Cola, Coke quickly countered with the boast that it was the "real thing." These two soft drink companies were rivals in the same marketplace, and they invested parallel sums in the same kinds of advertising. But Jews and Arabs are not rivals with a common purpose. While the Arabs intend to destroy the Jewish state and the idea of Jewish peoplehood, Jews have a *disincentive* to enter the war of words. They want recognition and acceptance from the very rulers and people who attack them. Why should any Jew, even the most ardent of Zionists, consecrate his life to the denunciation of Arab imperialism if he wants nothing from the Arabs but peace? Hoping that the Arabs will turn friendly "if not tomorrow then the day after," in the words of a popular Hebrew song, Israel and its supporters are genuinely disinclined to answer the propaganda against them, much less strike back in kind, lest by exacerbating tensions "they only make things worse."

The disinclination goes much deeper—to the heart of our liberal hopes. I use the collective pronoun because whatever our voting record or political affiliation most people in democratic countries are "liberal" in the sense that I have defined the term earlier—being committed to a rational and peaceful approach to political questions, to the benefits of pluralism and an open society, to individual freedom and individual rights. The hopefulness about human nature that underlies these positions means that we have a considerable stake in imagining the Arabs to be every bit as reasonable, as kindly, as peaceable, and as tolerant as ourselves.

When liberal optimism is confronted by determined aggression, either it admits the reality of aggression and suspends its belief that the world *is* liberal for long enough to help make it so, or it maintains its liberal optimism and denies the reality of aggression. The conditional or skeptical liberal will respond to the threat of assault by demanding the right of self-defense in a "just war" and by preparing for extended battle. The liberal fundamentalist, contrarily, is one for whom liberalism is less a political preference than an ontological principle. He must therefore deny the aggression that contradicts his belief.

The term liberal fundamentalism yokes two words that stand in sharpest historic opposition. Liberal originally denoted someone open-minded and free from prejudice, "favorable to constitutional changes and legal or administrative reforms tending in the direction of freedom and democracy" (this and more from the Oxford Unabridged). Liberal was the antonym of fundamentalist, a recently coined term for the religious arch-conservative. Yet by now, liberalism is itself far enough advanced to have produced its own fundamentalist faithful, who do not acknowledge the inflexibility of their beliefs.

Liberals who transpose the religious convictions of an earlier age into a modern secular–political ideology may stand in the same relation to the fundamental tenets of their credo as any other fundamentalists. They may deny the reality of political evil with the unshakable conviction of forebears who either proclaimed or denied original sin. There is always a potential point of collusion between the aggressor, who wants to conceal his intention in order to execute it effectively, and the liberal fundamentalist, who has to deny aggression so that he can continue to believe that humans were created in *his* image.

This proclivity for self-deception in modern democratic societies was described by Jean-Francois Revel in *How Democracies Perish*. Almost everything that Revel says about the reluctance and failure of democratic peoples and governments to stand up to Communism into the mid-1980s—the "fear of knowing" what it is too painful to know; the adoption of a double standard favoring the enemy; the denial of aggressive impulses in the enemy and their attribution to oneself—applies to the situation we are here investigating. Revel writes: "Democracy is by its very nature turned inward. Its vocation is the patient and realistic improvement of life in a community. . . . Democracy tends to ignore, even deny, threats to its existence because it loathes doing what is needed to counter them. It awakens only when the danger becomes deadly, imminent, evident. By then, either there is too little time left for it to save itself, or the price of survival has become crushingly high."

Happily, these predictions did not prove true for France and England and America. The unanticipated collapse of Communism postponed any immediate threat to those democracies, at least from the aggressive Communism that Revel feared would crush them. But the Arab countries are not likely to collapse in any analogous way, and the democratic state of Israel lacks NATO's strength. If Revel thought the great democracies unlikely to muster the political will to stand up to Communist belligerence, Israel, facing much greater odds without any military coalition like NATO to defend it, is much more prone than they were to weaken in the face of persistent aggression.

Revel observes that democratic civilization was the first in history to blame itself because another power was working to destroy it. He could have found in the Jews a much earlier example of a civilization that blamed itself because other powers were working to destroy it. As we have already suggested, the high ratio in Jewish civilization of self-blame over self-praise has always encouraged individual morality at the expense of political self-confidence. Confrontation with a civilization that reverses these proportions may well prove fatal, especially if the Jews are without tactical or regional allies. If democratic civilization is so reluctant to stand up for itself, how much less inclined will it be to stand up for a distant country and how much more inclined to blame that fellow democracy for the aggression levelled against it.

The liberal reflexes of democratic societies help to explain the otherwise astonishing discrepancy between the failure of liberal public opinion to publicize the massacre of the Jews in the 1940's and the obsessive preoccupation of that same liberal sector with Israel's misdeeds since the 1970's. In World War II it was necessary for liberals to obscure German intentions, which required the suppression of news about the war against the Jews. German atrocities were too horrible to contemplate, and if acknowledged, would have required fighting the war on an additional front. That the allies were not ready to bomb the approach routes to Auschwitz, even when the worst was already known, tells us how unprepared they were to confront the Nazi war against the Jews.

In the case of the Arab war against the Jewish state, obscuring Arab intentions requires identifying Jews as the cause of the conflict. By blaming Israel for Arab complaints, liberals anticipate a reasonable, pacific solution to the conflict. Political pressure can be brought to bear on Israel to force the small Jewish polity to come to terms; it is much harder to influence the Arabs. The democratic Jewish state is subject to "rational" persuasion; not so the Arabs. The more determinedly and, by Western standards, irrationally, Arab governments and their agents pursue their anti-Israel campaign, and the more violent and distorting the instruments of their aggression, the more desperately the liberal imagination tries to blame the Jews for incurring Arab displeasure.

The notion of Jewish responsibility for Arab rejectionism is almost irresistibly attractive to liberals, because the truth otherwise seems so bleak. To face Arab intentions as the Israelis have been doing for almost half a century is to pay the price that Israelis have to pay through a life of unparalleled disciplined vigilance. They must not only consecrate much of their lives to self-defense, but what is infinitely more difficult, demand of their children and grandchildren increasing levels of national service.

Well-wishers elsewhere are under no parallel constraint. Arab belligerence does not threaten them or their families.

The Demonization of Israel

When people outside Israel, fully convinced that the Arabs *must* be as conciliatory as some of their spokesmen are prepared to say they are, urge the "return of land for peace" to governments that obviously prefer land over peace, they don't for a moment intend to sacrifice the targeted victim—any more than the very same kinds of people did in the 1930s when they gave the very same optimistic appraisals of German civilization and Communist egalitarianism. Their faith dictates that they hold Jews responsible for the refusal of the Arabs to accept Israel, because liberal hopes can be realized through the Jews alone. This is the crux of the matter: Arab governments and leaders and insurrectionists are not liberal.

The modern Jew is thus resaddled with the double burden he has carried through all but a fraction of this century; in becoming the target of the most determined aggressors, he unwittingly aggresses against the liberal faith. Because his enemy wants his extinction, he becomes an affront to those who insist on tolerance and pacification. The hatred that Jews inspire among their enemies—for compelling political reasons—reminds liberals that enmity is real and that it has great generative energy. No one is grateful to the Jews for this reminder. Anti-Semitism involves the displacement of rage, and blaming the Jews displaces fear of that rage.

Since democratic society does not want to perceive itself as heartless or collaborationist, those who court favor with the Arabs have to deny the war against the Jewish state or else justify their betrayal of the Jews in a language of moral convenience. The tilt toward the Arabs has the code name of even-handedness. A false symmetry is established between Jews and Arabs as in the term "the Arab-Israeli conflict." Having once redefined the Arab war against Israel as merely another regional dispute over territory—like the Iran–Iraq war, for example, or the war between Argentina and Britain over control of the Falkland Islands—politicians pretend that there is nothing greater at stake than the relative size of a country, and that favoring Jews or Arabs is only a matter of political preference between two more or less parallel peoples with similar political aims. A policy of even-handedness based on this artificial symmetry can justify arms deals and alliances with Arab states without compunction over the consequence of such deals for Israel.

Still, neutrality between so large a concentration of powers and so vulnerable a people would seem unfair to the smaller. This is where the Arab moral inversion becomes so tempting. Ascribing to Israel the blame for its predicament, democratic countries can pursue their self-interest free of any lingering moral scruple. Israel is examined for its every moral failing to justify policies of disengagement, while the moral failings of Arab countries are considered no one's business but their own, so that their blatant abuses of human rights should not get in the way of realpolitik. The notorious double standard is applied to the weaker, democratic country that already has the highest standards of human rights in the region, and, considering its permanent siege, perhaps the highest relative record of human rights in the world. It is not applied to the countries at the bottommost rungs of the same moral scale.

Thus, the turn against Israel is one of the few issues in the

The Demonization of Israel

United States that appeals equally to the ideological Right and the ideological Left, no less today than in the 1930s. When President Bush discredits Israel for the sake of closer ties with Arab oil states, he is warmly congratulated by the *New York Times* liberal columnist Anthony Lewis. Before Pat Buchanan charged Jewish supporters of Israel with anti-Americanism during the Republican presidential primary race of 1992, the same charge had been leveled by Gore Vidal in *The Nation*. Suspicion of Israel and its supporters unites the left wing of the Democratic party with the right wing of the Republicans, much as communist anti-Zionism once mirrored German racism in denying the legitimacy of a Jewish people. Whereas the propaganda war against the Jews was waged in the 1930s from two separate directions, Arab opposition to Israel combines the two approaches. It threatens through combined Arab power and moralizes through the plight of the abandoned Palestinians. The Arab propaganda war offers both sides of the political spectrum the opportunity of pursuing their ideological and practical goals while blaming the Jews for being the Arab target.

Thus far we have described the durability of anti-Semitism in politics and the way it challenges the moral convictions of those who call themselves liberal. As the test case of liberalism, the Jews themselves are torn between the desire to see its promise realized through the defense of their rights and regret for the suspension of optimism that defense of their rights requires. Exacerbating the problem for the Jews is their geographic division into two main communities: the one under physical attack for its life, the other under psychological attack for defending the first. American Jews may continue to lead the struggle for the security of Israel, or they may join in the liberal betrayal of the hard-won Jewish state. Arab rejectionism with its increasingly sophisticated propaganda has long since begun to undermine not only the political resolve of some American Jews, but even the self-confidence of many Israelis.

Chapter Six

The Ugly Israeli

From the beginning of the modern period, anti-Jewish politics subjected the Jews to a particular kind of strain. Wherever anti-Semitism became a significant component of the new nationalistic or the old conservative politics, modernizing Jews were virtually forced into the alternative liberal camp. But whereas French liberals, German liberals, and Polish liberals expressed liberalism in their own language, on their own soil, and as part of the secularization and political evolution of their own nations, the liberalizing Jew had to make the transition from Jewish (religious) jurisdiction to French or German or Polish (secular) citizenship in tension between his own people and another. The move outward—which required if not virtual abandonment of Jewish language, culture, and tradition, at least some modification of

Jewishness through acculturation—remained ultimately dependent for its reception on the dominant group.

Jean-Paul Sartre noted in his work *Anti-Semite and Jew* that where the welcome was not forthcoming, anti-Semitism could push the Jew back on himself, and force him to be "authentic" through a reaffirmation of his identity. Sartre himself had been confronted with the problem of French anti-Semitism during World War II when the collaborationist government of Vichy actively assisted the Nazis in their round-up of Jews, and his book was a belated attempt to deal directly with the issue of Jew-hatred that French intellectuals earlier had denied or ignored. However, as many Jewish critics noted when the book appeared, Sartre's notion of reflexive authenticity is partially demeaning to the very Jews it seeks to protect. It ignores the authenticity of Jewish civilization, which does not depend for its confirmation on anyone else's judgment, and, conversely, it demeans those Jews whose decision to quit the Jewish people may be a matter of informed choice. It is as though Jean-Paul Sartre had defined Frenchness as the necessary reaction to xenophobic Germans, ignoring the independent generative powers of a French identity and the possibility of a Frenchman choosing to become some other national by choice. The analogy is improbable not so much because of the differences in Jewish and French national identity as because of the hatred that disfigured the Jew to the point that he would so often aspire to assume an identity not his own. Sartre touched on what is perhaps the most painful of all the legacies of anti-Semitism —the way it renders the Jews unnatural, then hates them all the more for being untrue to their own people.

The Ugly Israeli

A great many European Jews tried to escape the ignominy of anti-Semitism through conversion. Before the modern period, and in Russia until the Revolution, a Jew who wished to quit his people had to convert to Christianity, which made the choice more painful but in no way affected the boundaries between Jew and non-Jew. After Emancipation, the promise of equality raised hopes of acceptance in the Jews while the concurrent rise of anti-Semitism increased their insecurity. Offered the possibility of citizenship, modern Jews less often converted to Christianity than identified with the liberal politics and outlook that had sought their advancement. If they were then still unwelcome, they often blamed the Jew in themselves for having alienated the liberal, or tried to mitigate opposition to themselves by dividing the "good" Jews from "bad." Early Jewish reformers of the Enlightenment blamed anti-Semitism on the reactionary dress and practices of the Hasidic Jews; Jewish socialists blamed anti-Semitism on the Jews who had agreed to play the role of middlemen in feudal societies and on Jewish capitalists who took over their role as exploiters; Jewish assimilationists blamed anti-Semitism on the false consciousness of nationalist Jews who refuse to melt into the mainstream. Anti-Semites got it wrong as usual when they accused Jews of betraying their countries of citizenship as a consequence of their "dual loyalty." From the dawn of Emancipation until the present, the conflict of loyalties that anti-Semitism forces upon the Jews resulted almost exclusively in their betrayal not of Gentiles but of fellow Jews.

Now, in chilling duplication of the past, anti-Zionism affects Jewish attitudes toward Israel precisely the way anti-

Semitism once affected Jewish attitudes toward Jewishness. When Arabs began to attack the legitimacy of Israel, they forced liberal Jews, including liberal Israelis, to choose between confidence in the Jewish state and confidence in the triumph of liberalism. Under political pressure that has grown steadily stronger over the past twenty years, many Israelis tried responding to the charges against them by differentiating between "two Zionisms," the pure and good Zionism of ingathering versus the evil Zionism of expansionism. Despite the transforming presence of a Jewish country, intellectuals and writers in Israel today, like their diaspora counterparts of the 1930s, try to separate their own "progressive" desire for an independent homeland from the "reactionary" desires of their fellow Jews, in order to escape the Arab politics of hatred.

I open a Hebrew murder mystery and begin to read for pleasure. The book starts promisingly on a late winter morning: "Jerusalem on Sabbath was quiet, and the neighborhood through which he was passing, normally quiet, was now altogether asleep." The discovered corpse on this otherwise calm Sabbath is a teaching analyst whose murder is linked to the mysterious workings of the psychoanalytic profession. The plot and the writing are just about good enough to keep me going. But then I catch the first unmistakable whiff of rot. An Arab worker on hospital grounds adjoining the murder site accidentally finds the murder weapon but is afraid to report it because of the danger to which this will expose him. He knows that being Arab will make him the target of suspicion that would never be directed against a Jew. And then, as predictable as the mystery genre

The Ugly Israeli

itself, the turn of the author's political mind: The chief suspect is an Israeli army captain who had consulted the psychoanalyst for impotence incurred as a result of the torture he was forced to practice on Arab prisoners. He is suspected of killing his doctor to protect his future in the army. A book without any other hint of social commentary—a book that could otherwise be set as readily as Reykjavik as Rehavia— frames a symmetry of the maligned Arab and the Jewish torturer, who though innocent of murdering the analyst is guilty of the more heinous crime, the one being committed against Arabs in the name of the state.

The author may have meant to redeem this ugly Israeli by according him a conscience. His prick rebels at the blood that his hand has shed. Or rather, the author acts as his conscience, unmanning him for having committed the national crime. Here in America, the ugly Israeli is no longer accorded any such moral twinge: he is a torturer whose manhood swells at the blood the hand is shedding. In an American potboiler called *Pattern Crimes*, for example, a cabal of Israeli right-wing zealot, Christian fundamentalist, Mossad officer, and Jerusalem policeman organizes to blow up the Dome of the Rock. The group not only kills a number of innocent people who might have exposed their plan but also mutilates the bodies for good measure, following the custom of a "special Israeli commando unit" that used the same technique in its murder of Palestinians. They also cut up the breasts of the women, being equal opportunity butchers. At the end of the book when the ringleader kills himself, he is acknowledging merely the failure of his plan, not any regret.

Israeli writing will probably not go this far. Impossible to speak of mutilated corpses in Israel without causing unnecessary anguish to friends and relatives of those who met with this fate. Not that some writers would refrain from accusing their fellow Jews of such acts of barbarism, but any mention of mutilation in Israel would remind readers of the immoderate practices of their Arab neighbours, which it is not in their political interest to invoke. If I not mistaken, this subject in Israel is all but taboo.

Back in the 1950s and 1960s, during the years of grace when Israel and the Jews seemed on the point of being granted international acceptance, the popular myth of Israel was packaged for Americans by the novelist Leon Uris. The best-selling *Exodus* and its film adaptation starring Paul Newman probably marked the high point of Jewish popularity, making it hard to separate the poor quality of the book from its successful championship of the Jews. Whether because no great Israeli novel ever attempted to dramatize the rise of the Jewish state on quite such a large scale, or because the formulaic American best-seller discovering in the rise of Israel a new subject of splendid scope could exploit it with maximal effectiveness, *Exodus* was the best international advertisement the Jews had ever had. In its *samizdat* Russian version it was actually said to have sparked the national resurgence of Jews in the Soviet Union.

Nevertheless, as we can see more clearly in retrospect than we could at the time, Uris's pitch for Israel was based, like Jean-Paul Sartre's expose of anti-Semitism, less on an understanding of the Jews than on their reflection in the eyes of non-Jews. The main plot of the book, about the evolving love of the American Gentile nurse Kitty Freeman (who is "as American as apple pie") for the Israeli-born Ari Ben Canaan, makes the validation of the Jews dependent on the approval of the Gentiles. Only because Kitty Freeman gradually comes to appreciate the depth of Jewish victimization and the heights of Jewish bravery and to adopt Israel's cause—in the form of an actual Jewish child—is the reader expected to applaud the ability of the fledgling state to survive against its enemies. Thus, ironically, the book that did most for the image of the Jews actually turns out to be about the *image* of the Jews, an image of tight-lipped tough-guy masculinity that is freely adapted from the American western and has about as much to do with the Jews of Israel as Hamlet had to do with Denmark. When Uris was confronted one day with the testimony of the captain of the refugee ship that had tried to run the British blockade in 1947—testimony which contradicted the version in *Exodus*—he said, "How many people have heard of him and how many have heard of me?" The implication would seem to be that his version must be truer because it had reached more people. He had exploited the idea of Israel's victimization at the moment of its greatest trendiness and by reducing the complexity of Jewish history to a pulp fiction formula had put the product within easy reach.

Given the woodenness of Uris's fictional sabras, one can readily understand why it was so refreshing in the late 1960s to begin reading the nuanced, finely textured works of genuine Israeli authors, particularly those who were breaking away from the founding myths of the country to explore questions of moral ambiguity. A short story called "The Prisoner" appearing in one of the first English anthologies of Israeli writing seemed much more profound than its companion works about wounded veterans and embattled kibbutz farmers because it opened the sore of self-doubt. Set during Israel's War of Independence, the story describes a detail of Israeli soldiers who take a poor Arab shepherd prisoner for no better reason than that they are embarrassed to return from their mission empty-handed. They subject their prisoner to great indignities. The narrator who is a member of the unit marvels at the callousness of his compatriots:

> And there were some who had steady jobs, some who were on their way up in the world, some who were hopeless cases to begin with, and some who rushed to the movies and all the theatres and read the week-end supplements of two newspapers. And there were some who knew long passages from Horace and the Prophet Isaiah and from Chaim Nachman Bialik and even from Shakespeare; some who loved their children and their wives and their slippers and the little gardens at the sides of their houses; some who hated all forms of favoritism, insisted that each man keep his proper place in line, and raised a hue and cry at the slightest suspicion of discrimination; some whose inherent good-nature had been permanently soured by the thought of paying the rent and taxes; some who were not at all what they seemed and some who were exactly what they seemed. There they all stood, in a happy circle around the blindfolded prisoner, who at that very moment extended a calloused hand (one never knows if it's dirty, only that it's the hand of a peasant) and said to them: "Fi, cigara?" A cigarette?

The Ugly Israeli

Many strands of sensitivity are interwoven in this set piece of reflection: the sensitive writer's indictment of his bourgeois countrymen; the sensitive soldier's revolt against the abuses of war; and the sensitive Jew's protest against mistreatment of the stranger, who was also the native, in his midst. Actually, this story touched off something of a cultural revolution in Israel. One of the first works of post-independence fiction to train its critical eye on the struggle that had attained that independence, it featured a narrator sufficiently estranged from his society to puncture its accepted ideas, a soldier in a country at war who questions the manner in which that war is being waged and, by implication, his country's reliance on force in the pursuit of its destiny. From the standpoint of contemporary western fiction this was less a breakthrough than an adoption of the prescribed adversarial posture of the modern writer toward bourgeois democratic society. But whereas our societies had long since sustained a literature antagonistic to their ideals and mores, this adversarial Israeli literature, because the founding ideology of the country was still so young and so strong, had the force of a son's stinging slap against his father's face.

Although S. Yizhar may be one of the pioneering stylists of modern Israeli fiction, this particular story of the prisoner is so artificial that you know the author himself was not convinced it had ever happened, certainly not in the way he had written it. Were the above scene authentic, the author would not have had to overstuff it rhetorically as he does. When I first read the story, I would have said what many good people would still say about it today, that the author indicted his countrymen because he was worried for their soul. No doubt there were plenty of ugly incidents during the successive wars against the Arabs, and this fable of ordinary citizens transformed into heartless persecutors would help to warn against abuses of power—of which all men are equally capable, and of which the Jews too must stand forewarned now that they were soldiers.

When I first read the story, I regretted that its aesthetic merit fell so far below what I took to be its moral grasp. But actually the one derived from the other, the forced rhetoric from the pseudomorality. The real problem facing those Israeli soldiers was not their desire to humiliate Arab shepherds. The Jewish society Yizhar was describing had been prodded into battle very much against its will by the refusal of Arab rulers, who spoke in the name of Arab shepherds, to accept the idea of a Jewish land. And if these reluctant soldiers were ungentlemanly or even cruel in their self-defense, their action had to be assessed against the circumstance of its commission.

Thus, the moral problem in Yizhar's story was a comforting diversion from the one that truly gripped the Jews. By omitting the political premise of the story, the author had presented its action in a false light, much as propaganda does when it moves in for the kill without full disclosure of the facts. What those soldiers had to ask themselves in the period of the story and ever since is whether they would have the stamina as relatively tolerant and conciliatory human beings to hold out against aggressive political enemies lacking corresponding tolerance. Yizhar had trivialized the Israelis, cutting them to fit the popular mold of soldier-villains without admitting the much deeper anxiety of their unique situation. German soldiers or European villagers may have hounded the innocent Jew because the government speaking for them wanted to rid their country of his presence. These Jewish soldiers were in arms against the Arabs who similarly wanted to rid this country of *their* presence. Focus on the innocent Arab shepherd to the exclusion of the hostile Arab autocrats distorted the moral context of Jewish behavior, sentimentalizing the whole question of good and evil.

It was precisely this falsification that admitted Israeli literature into the liberal—leftist cultural mainstream of the West, and koshered its writers with "the better kind of reader" for whom the best selling *Exodus* was political as well as literary junk. I don't mean to suggest, not even slightly, that this was Yizhar's consideration in writing the story. As the historians and critics of Israeli literature point out, reaction against the Zionist myth was virtually inevitable on the part of the native-born Israelis who took their birthright for granted, and the artistic rebellion of a younger generation against the heroic phase of Israeli writing was to be expected as a matter of course. Yet this particular kind of revision of the Zionist myth held enormous appeal for certain people outside the country, who had never felt comfortable with a Jewish national state in the first place and who valued criticism of it for supplying them with a moral excuse to denounce rather than defend it.

The American Jewish writer Henry Roth wrote in 1963, "I feel that to the great boons Jews have already conferred upon humanity, Jews in America might add this last and greatest one: of orienting themselves toward ceasing to be Jews." Although Henry Roth changed his mind following the

Six-Day War of 1967, many of his former leftist colleagues continued to regard the Zionist movement as the blackest force of reaction, and younger Jews of the New Left took up the opposition to Jewish nationhood at the very moment that Roth made his peace with it. Had Israel become merely another country from the moment of its founding, as Italy did after the risorgimento, this opposition would have evaporated, since there would have been no further reason for Jews to join in defaming it. But the Arabs deprived the Jews of this historical possibility. When they refueled the war against Israel and Zionism to keep alive the question of Israel's contingency, a new generation of Jewish radicals did just what Henry Roth had done in his youth in response to the Jew-blame of the 1930s on the part of radicals and Communist fellow travelers. They advertised their defection from their discredited tribe as a higher form of allegiance to internationalist ideals.

Jewish liberals, though less distressed than the radicals by a Jewish national state, inclined to identify Jewishness with political weakness, which meant—as I heard from a Polish Jewish intellectual in 1985—"identification with the beaten against the beaters." Embarrassed by the tribal call to rally around a Jewish country with Jewish laws and a Jewish government, such Jews could justify the "chauvinistic" support of their fellow Jews only if Israel were perceived as an oppressed victim. Thus the military strength of Israel, which protected its Jewish inhabitants from certain extinction, was proof that Israel had lost its claim to their moral protection.

Israeli literature of self-affirmation had about as much chance of pleasing these Jews as the Kronstadt revolt of 1921 could have impressed Leon Trotsky with its aspirations of political independence. Bialik's deep national pathos, Agnon's intricate Jewish fables, Alterman and Shlonsky's consolidation of a modern-classical Hebrew verse, the early novels of kibbutz trial and error, ingathered exiles, Jerusalem atmosphere—the more deeply the new Israeli literature reached into its unique experience and sources, the more alien it would seem to Jews who wanted to remain true to their leftist and liberal faiths.

A story like "The Prisoner," on the other hand, was laudably familiar. It not only discredited the national myth and the bourgeois polity but showed that the dissident intellectual tradition could function as powerfully in a Jewish country as it had in Europe and America. To young Israelis the story must have been the most *reassuring* news they had ever received, internalizing as it did the danger to the country. The story suggested that it was their moral standard which was corrupting the innocent Arabs rather than vice versa, and who would not rather confront his own questionable morality than the ferocity of an intransigent adversary? As for the Jewish readers abroad—each of us with at least some irreducible dot, or (in Yiddish) *pintele,* of liberal-leftism in our souls—we now had a sample of Israeli literature reflecting the accepted ideas of our culture instead of the forbidding Zionist challenge to uproot ourselves in spirit and body. Small wonder that the Israeli writers and intellectuals who moved decisively onto this track gained more attention abroad the more they challenged Zionist assumptions.

Notice, however, that at this early stage the Israeli writer still presented the ugly Israeli in the image of EveryJew.

Yizhar is embarrassingly dogmatic about pervasiveness of cruelty among his fellows. The very point of his indictment is to accuse all alike; guilt was attached to the sins of Jewish soldiering, period.

And to the Jewish presence in Palestine, period. It was in 1963, well within the borders of little Israel, that A. B. Yehoshua wrote his fable, "Facing the Forests," about the floundering history student who undertakes to guard the forests of the Jewish National Fund and ends by abetting the Arab in burning them to the ground. This was another work that seemed to defy the norms of both Israeli fiction and Israeli society by subverting the national myth. Through the dawning perception of the student, the reader is invited to appreciate that the Israeli forest—symbol of the healthful pioneering effort—covers what had once been an Arab village. The mute Arab who still lives in the forest with a frightened child resents its usurpation to the point of hatred, and if he cannot have his home back, he intends to deny it to another. The student experiences such an extreme moral crisis when he begins to see himself through the Arab's eyes that he considers assisting the Arab in an act of arson. Short of that, he is exhilarated when the forest is finally set aflame. "Pines split and crash. Wild excitement sweeps him, rapture. He is happy. Where is the Arab now? The Arab speaks to him out of the fire, wishes to say everything, everything and at once. Will he understand?"

The Arab of "Facing the Forests" is portrayed like Yizhar's prisoner at the mercy of the Israeli conqueror. And again at issue is the capacity of the Jew to identify with the position of the Arab victim. Where God once spoke to Moses from the flaming bush, the Arab now speaks to the Jew out of the fire. God had said to the Jews, live, which left open the thorny question of how they ought to live. The Arab said to the Jews, leave, which takes no great skill to decipher or, for that matter, to obey. If the new Jewish morality was to be based on heeding the message from the fire, then the Jews had only to leave the land of Israel to regain their innocence. Neither the author nor his protagonist, the student of history, is prepared to say as did the biblical Israelites, *naaseh venishma*, we will obey and heed this counsel. But Yehoshua does believe in the moral sensitivity of the Israeli who is sympathetic to the Arab's protest.

Do you? In the story the Arab gives vent to the student's repressed desires when he sets the Jewish forest aflame. If we apply to Yehoshua the same kind of psychoanalyzing to which he routinely subjects his society, we would have to say that the Arab gangs who began burning down the forests during the Intifada were acting out his suppressed desires to have the guilty state destroyed. What is guilt if not a desire for punishment? If the Jews feel they have wronged the Arabs by planting trees on what were once their villages, doesn't their moral sensitivity require them to conspire with the Arabs to have themselves punished?

But if Arabs and Jews are expected to observe the same code of human behavior, the moral weight of the story falls in the wrong place, much as it does in Yizhar's story of the prisoner. During our lifetime, Jewish children by the hundreds of thousands were stripped of everything that was theirs by right and driven from the lands of their birth where their forebears had lived for centuries. Were they and their guardians to behave like the Arabs in the story, they would have to devote their lives to reclaiming their lost patrimony, or at the very least to prevent its use by others. Israelis, even including Yehoshua, never pressed the land claims of the hordes of Jews who were driven from Arab countries where their families had lived at least as long as the Arab's family had lived in Palestine. How, then, can he accept the undying grudge of the Arabs against him?

Moral relativism leads to dangerous ends. If Jews credit the Arabs with dignity for nursing their hatred, then Jews who have been robbed of so much more than Arabs and humiliated so much longer and more deeply ought to be dignified too, and keep their matches dry to kindle their flinty hearts. If honor, grievance, vengeance, and violence are considered values in Arabs, then they must be considered values to the same degree in other human beings, Jews included. Alternately, if Jews are expected to adapt to new political realities, to forfeit the property of generations for the chance to begin anew, to abandon graves, and synagogues, not to speak of properties and rights, and to count themselves fortunate for having escaped with their lives, we can surely expect the same of Arabs, creatures of God like the Jews, and currently blessed with more riches and lands than most other people on earth.

Although no work of fiction should be reduced to its message or moral, A. B. Yehoshua's story has often been taught and dramatized for Israeli youth and military recruits to raise their social consciousness. Indeed, when the student in the story perceives that the Jew and the Arab have traded places in history, the narrative encourages the reader to perceive it in the same way. But the transposition is false.

The Ugly Israeli

Whatever Israeli writers may wish to pretend, the Jew remains at the mercy of a civilization that, unlike his, still measures power by the size of its conquests. Israelis will have to go a long way before they have internalized the Arab values of land and honor, and until they do, the Israeli writer distorts both the historical record and any universal principle of morality by claiming an imperial status he has not earned.

I'm reminded of a Jewish joke. Transported one Yom Kippur by the need to repent of his sins, the rabbi prostrates himself before the Ark, shouting, "Dear God, forgive me, I am as nothing before Your Glory!" The cantor, infected by this enthusiasm, echoes, "O Lord, I am nothing, dust and ashes, before Your Holy Throne." Even the president is moved to follow the rabbi's example, declaring his abject worthlessness. Finally the poor synagogue beadle feels he must show his piety and hurls himself to the ground. "I am nothing, a mere nothing, a worm." But this proves too much for the congregants, who protest: "Look who thinks he's a nothing!" If the world had a sense of humor it would be holding its sides with laughter at the Israelis who allow themselves to be compared—by Arabs!—to the Crusaders and the Suleimans. Conquerors don't have a conscience. That is why many Arabs, facing the forests, feel that time is on their side.

But I'm straying from the point, which is that these stories ascribed guilt to the sins of Jewish soldiering and Jewish conquest without reference to the amount of land involved. Since these works were written before 1967, such scruples as Israelis felt about their national legitimacy had to be attached to Israel entire, to the narrow strip of land that no matter how small was still too big in the eyes of its Arab neighbors. Whatever the sources of their anxiety, Israeli writers could not attribute their dilemma or their disquiet to partisan politics within Israel. *That* temptation could only be realized after the Six-Day War, the War of Attrition, and the Yom Kippur War of 1973 had resulted in a larger territory. Although there were no Arab claimants for peace except the munificently rewarded Anwar Sadat, and though Arab rejectionists had yet to accept the Israeli reality, that "occupied" land was a window of opportunity for writers and intellectuals who wanted to free themselves from blame for the national predicament. They could now attempt to make a moral distinction between the ugly Israeli expansionist and the good Jews who were prepared to "return land for peace." Eventually, some of the writers even made explicit their courtship of Western liberal opinion by publishing letters in the leading American newspapers urging Americans to mobilize political pressure against Israel in order to force on Israelis policies that their fellow citizens were too benighted or too wicked to appreciate.

In anticipation of accidental or deliberate misinterpretation, let me clarify this point. Of course, a legitimate argument could have been made for yielding the territories. In the immediate aftermath of the Six-Day War the vast majority of Israelis expected that the Arabs would sue for peace to recover the disputed territories, and in keeping with those expectations, the Sinai was given to Egypt as part of the peace treaty of 1978. The legitimate argument for yielding territory accepts the risk of territorial disadvantage in the hope that it will improve the prospects of Arab tolerance of

The Ugly Israeli

Israel. The argument is mendacious, however, when it pretends that the size of Israel has anything to do with the Arab war against it. (The stories cited above remind us of just how false it is.) The argument is also illegitimate when it claims that the failure to take such a risk is immoral. There can be nothing moral, least of all at the end of the twentieth century, in the readiness of Jewish parents to wager the lives of their children against their hopes of Arab moderation, and there can be nothing inherently moral in the Jewish assessment of what constitutes a political risk. Thus, while the writers in question had every right to propose political solutions for their country, they lied in pretending that these solutions were moral alternatives to a callous Zionism.

Kafka would not have made this mistake. Kafka took his own moral failings very seriously, but without ever ascribing truer morality to the plaintiffs who charged him with sin. Once God is no longer recognized as the Father and Judge of the universe, guilt may be just a reflexive response to authority in any guise, wicked or benevolent, bogus or real. In the modern court where the (Jewish) defendant is guilty by virtue of being charged, the man who tries to prove his innocence is doomed, and deservedly so. Joseph K., charged one fine morning with an unspecified crime, becomes the accomplice of his accusers when lacking any knowledge of the court he answers its indictment. The victim of Kafka's *The Trial* is not permitted any more sympathy than the executioner, for where there is no legitimate and fair court, the man who answers a summons collaborates in his victimization.

In *The Trial* written during World War I, Kafka puts on trial the liberal faith that so many of his contemporaries had substituted for the Jewish faith—the belief that human reason would cultivate a kindlier society than religious authority had tried to impose in the name of God. Lacking all the inherited cultural trappings of a religious civilization that allowed many Yiddish and Hebrew writers to feel the protection of a divine justice long after they had disclaimed its authority, Kafka placed himself under pitiless scrutiny. He hated the guilt that tormented him, which derived from a father in whom he had long since ceased to trust and whom he despaired of pleasing. By the same light, he exposed the phony guilt of those who continued to justify themselves to an unreliable idea of authority, whether human or divine. If literature really had the kind to power that some of us in our youth ascribed to it, Kafka would have squeezed from the Jews the last drop of self-pity, which grows from their lingering belief that their vulnerability constitutes a modern species of martyrdom.

Nor would the Russian Jew Isaac Babel have fallen into this error. Babel, as different from Kafka as Odessa is from Prague, subjected his own Jewish humanist yearnings to equally merciless scrutiny, by the naked light of the sun as compared to Kafka's welling insights of the night. In order to know first-hand the violence that was the ontological principle of his revolutionary age, Babel learned to ride with the Cossacks who detested the peace-loving Jews. He, almost alone among modern Jewish authors, penetrated the society of his antagonists to discover the sources of their contempt and to feel the moral life as they felt it. This was not done out of Jewish self-loathing. If anything, Babel was able through the expanded moral vision he acquired among the Cossacks to represent the dogged courage of Jewish yearners-for-goodness, of an intellectual like himself with specs on his nose and autumn in his heart. But never did he attempt to wrap the Cossacks and the Jews in the imaginary cloak of human brotherliness so as to obscure the differences between them—neither to satisfy the egalitarian directives of the Revolution nor his own desire to be loved.

One of the final tales of Babel's *Red Cavalry*, written just after World War I, pronounces a harsh judgment on the modern Jewish intellectual. For a year Lyutov has ridden with the Cossacks, sacrificing his scruples to their code of behavior, and trying to prove himself a man on their terms. But still he is held in contempt. Now the Cossack whose horse had been arbitrarily assigned to him by the squadron commander returns in a murderous rage to reclaim it. Lyutov protests to the commander over this "gift" of a gratuitous foe: how was he to blame for the Cossack's hatred? The commander's fury explodes at this will to innocence:

"I see through you," he said. "I see right through you. You'd like not to have any enemies in life. Yes, that's what you keep trying to arrange for yourself—to have no enemies." Babel knew there was nothing wrong with the wish to have no enemies, or even with the obsessive wish to have no enemies. But his was also the artistic, indistinguishable from the moral, integrity to see the wish through the eyes of the surrounding majority that despised it. He does not ask us to applaud Lyutov's sweet Jewish soul without revealing how it was reviled and how it could be destroyed by those he was eager to claim as his brothers.

The modern Israeli writers who have been taken up with

mounting enthusiasm by the *New Yorker* and *New York Review of Books* show no such honesty. They "travel" among the Arabs to prove that the Jews have no enemies, or that such enemies as they have are strictly of their own making, or that the Jews and Arabs are so fundamentally alike as to mirror one another indistinguishably.

Take Amos Oz, reporting on a conversation with the editors of the East Jerusalem daily newspaper *Al-Fajr Al-Arabi* (*The Arab Dawn*), in his recent book *In the Land of Israel:*

> More than a hundred years ago, in 1868, in Vienna, Peretz Smolenskin founded a Zionist Hebrew journal that bore the same name as Abu Ziad's newspaper *The Dawn.*
>
> On the opening page of the first issue, Smolenskin wrote, "Neither in shame nor in disgrace do we believe . . . that the day will come and the kingdom will be restored . . . when like all peoples we shall not be ashamed of the desire to redeem our souls from the hands of strangers."
>
> It occurs to me that it is surely not difficult to translate those words into Arabic. And Ziad Abu Ziad would be only too happy to print them on the masthead of his *Dawn.* Is it right to compare; is it possible not to?

Before he reports on the actual conversation between himself and the Palestinian Arab editors, Amos Oz first sets up an artificial symmetry between Smolenskin's hyper-liberal European journal and the propaganda sheet of dogmatic nationalists, trying to turn the Arabs into the Jews he wants them to be. Although he seems to realize that his rhetorical questions (Is it right to compare the two *Dawns?* Is it possible not to compare them?) are no more than the pleas of a child to

make the world a fair playground because he does not want to
be hurt in it, he cannot give up the idea that both peoples are
fundamentally alike or the pretense that "over and above
reality [of the conflict between the Arabs and the Jews] float,
like a sweet cloud of hashish, the pleasures of piteousness and
self-indulgence. And in this the two opposing peoples are
indeed as similar as brothers." It comes as no surprise that
when the brotherly Arab editors found Oz's reportage in
print, they repudiated the interview, accusing him of having
softened their position. Remembering Lyutov's commander,
think what contempt these Arabs must feel for the Jewish
intellectuals who float "like a sweet cloud of hashish" in the
pleasures of their piteousness and self-indulgence.

Most of Amos Oz's account of his travels *In the Land of
Israel* is happily much more honest than this. However, he
has since been superceded in duplicity, and hence in liberal
popularity, by the younger David Grossman. The symmetry
between Arabs and Jews that Amos Oz is still a little
embarrassed to introduce, except by way of leading questions,
is taken by Grossman as the premise of his chronicle *The
Yellow Wind*. He devotes all his artistic powers to equating the
moral energy of the Arab desire for Palestine with the Jews'
age-old longing for Zion. When a sixteen-year-old Arab girl
talks to him about the city of Lod, "where the sky was always
blue," he does not remind her that she is sitting only a few
miles away but translates her nationalism into Jewish longing:

> I remembered the wistful lines of Yehuda Halevy, "The
> taste of your sand—more pleasant to my mouth than
> honey," and Bialik, who sang to the land which "the spring

eternally adorns," how wonderfully separation beautifies the beloved, and how strange it is, in the barrenness of the gray cement of [the Arab refugee camp] Deheisha, to hear sentences so full of lyric beauty, words spoken in a language more exalted than the everyday, poetic but of established routine, like a prayer or an oath: "And the tomatoes there were red and big, and everything came to us from the earth, and the earth gave us and gave us more."

Grossman does not even pay attention to his own evidence: the contrast between Yehuda Halevy who is prepared to find the sand as sweet as honey and the Arabs who imagine the land that they don't possess to be more magically fertile than the land they actually cultivate. It does not occur to him to ask why, if there is such symmetry in the nature of Jewish and Arab "longing," Arabs should now be in possession of 250,000 square miles while the Jews have a mere 8,000, which Arabs still clamor to conquer. He is determined to prove equivalence—between the Arab boy playing on a comb and the fabled Jewish fiddler on the roof, between the Arab grandmother and his own Jewish *bobbenyu*. One might ask why Grossman should travel among Arabs at all when they are so undifferentiated from the folks back home, but that would be to miss the political purpose of the book of which establishing perfect symmetry between Arab and Jew is but a first necessary step.

Consider what has to be done if Israel is to be declared the violator of Arab rights. Geographic perspective must be erased and historical facts obscured. First, the map of the Middle East, where Israel occupies but .02 of the territory, must be reduced to Israel alone so that Israel figures as the sole and dominant regional power. (The map prefacing the English edition of *The Yellow Wind* does exactly this.) Next, and more critically, history must be reduced to the present, so that Israel can figure as the deliberate occupier of alien land. Preposterous in itself, the charge of Israeli criminality can be made to stick if the focus is thus narrowed and the clock stopped.

But writing for Israelis who know their geography and their history, Grossman must also erase the cultural difference between Arab and Jewish civilization, between the punishing self-discipline that kept the Jews, in the words of the philosopher Simon Rawidowicz, an "every-dying people," and the religio-political reach that has given the Arabs twenty-two modern states. He must Judaize the Arabs so that he can Arabize the Jews. Since his will to innocence requires that he have no enemies, he must hold his fellow Jews responsible for the enemies he has. "Who are these people who are able to harden their hearts so much against others and against themselves, over the course of an entire generation or two, and become the kindling of the historical process they desire?" Grossman asks. These people are not, according to Grossman, the Palestinian terrorists with their support stations in Libya but rather the Jewish settlers of Judaea and Samaria, to whom he ascribes all the intransigence, possessiveness, and hostility of which he absolves the Arabs. What passes for empathy with the Arabs is actually a hatred transferred to the adherents of Gush Emunim, who believe that Israel has a right to the disputed territories.

Grossman will go to any lengths to hitch a ride with the liberal tradition. He even breathes new life into the

Communist-Arab claim of the 1930s that the Zionists were imperialist occupiers of a colonized people by invoking an analogy with one of the classic texts of British anti-imperialism, George Orwell's story, "Shooting an Elephant." In this famous work, a former British police officer in Burma describes how the hatred of the natives for his uniform had once provoked him into committing the ugly and cowardly act of shooting an elephant "solely to avoid looking like a fool." Grossman interweaves passages of Orwell's tough prose into his own description of the Jewish military court at Nablus, where he claims he witnessed one miscarriage of justice after another against the Palestinian Arabs. He forces the parallel between the corrupt British imperialism of its day with the corrupt Jewish occupation of the West Bank—and the implicit parallel between that other writer and himself.

Comparing the two works illuminates the contrast between true and false art. Orwell through controlled narration takes upon "himself" as narrator of the story the brunt of hatred directed against his British uniform, exposing the harm of British imperialism at his own expense. Not the good intentions of British civilization are brought into question, but the consequences of trying to impose it on another people. By contrast, Grossman presents himself as the innocent humanitarian Jew who has come to expose the foul Jewish court, to whitewash his conscience at the expense of his criminal compatriots. Every point of the implied comparison is fake: Israel is not an imperial power holding sway in foreign lands over Burmese and Indian multitudes but itself the target of imperial nations that will not grant its right to exist. Unlike the British—and the Arabs—who have a sense of manly honor instilled in them through long centuries of military tradition, Jews have no military tradition at all; having made a virtue of playing the fool in history, they are only afraid of becoming the corpse. Orwell had one of the toughest political minds of his day. That he should be pressed into service by this kind of simpering wishfulness does him as great an injustice as it does the Jews.

But the self-debasement does not end even there. In a fastidious Tel Aviv avant-garde literary journal a poem appeared comparing the Zionist impulse not merely to the imperialist British but to the worst of the Russian czars:

> *Peter the Great*
> *paved the capital city Petersburg*
> *on the northern marshes*
> *over the bones of peasants.*
> *David Ben Gurion*
> *paved*
> *the Burma Road, bypassing*
> *the road to the capital city Jerusalem*
> *with the bones of boys from the Holocaust.*

This historical analogy is meant to recall for us that in his eagerness to break the Arab siege of Jerusalem in 1948, David Ben-Gurion sent into battle an untrained unit of survivors, boys who had arrived from Europe so recently they barely had been processed as immigrants. The episode happens to be one of the most painful in the history of the settlement of

Israel, and this poet is not the first to want to rescue the sacrifices of the "boys from the Holocaust" from the chilling anonymity of Zionist myth. A poem is precisely the small place where wounds can be probed and where a private claim can be pressed against the impersonality of national imperatives. Yet the comparison between Ben Gurion's mistaken judgment in a war that was fought to provide a shelter for these refugees with the csar's indifferent sacrifice of the lives of his serfs, paves the road of poetry with the bones of false moral distinctions. This is the more unfortunate, since moral and aesthetic distinctions are what poets in particular are expected to uphold. The most sensitive of Israeli writers may understandably resent the unfair burden of defense they bear as a result of the accident of their birth, but how twisted their art becomes when they try to fit the Jewish reality into the procrustean bed of liberal stereotypes! The argument for political integrity and artistic honesty happen to be one and the same. In literature as in politics, all the talent and charm in the world are no match for truth and moral courage.

Were they as honest as Babel and Kafka, these Israeli writers, instead of plying us with imprecise analogies, would confront the unprecedented and unique political experience of modern Jews who have not escaped the vilification of their foes despite their wholesale efforts at national self-transformation. But here we come up against the severe handicap of the Jewish writer who wants to describe his situation. Modern Jewish fiction has been hampered by its limited access to the experience of anti-Jews, while art can only master what it knows. Targeted as prey, the Jewish writer was normally incapable of depicting the whole of the world he inhabited because he did not form part of anti-Semitic society; running with the hares, he could not describe the hounds.

Although thousands of Jewish poets, writers, and memoirists bore witness to the persecution of European Jewry, those who wrote were least able to know how the Ukrainian felt who stuffed the stomachs of slaughtered Jews with feathers, what the Pole had learned that made him decide to boycott Jewish stores, how the Frenchman had arrived at his motto, "à bas les juifs," how the German had evolved who was examining the skin of Jews for the interesting lampshade that it might yield. Since Jews did not place their faith in Hitler as the savior of their people, Jewish writers could not dramatize the manic energy of the Nazis who sought salvation in their extinction. The cultural assumptions of Jews were often antithetical to those of their neighbours, so that they were prevented by both the nature and the angle of their cultural vision from knowing the hatred that consumed them. As a result, the art that Jews produced about their own history is dramatically skewed, and the dramatic bias is always in danger of slipping into moral bias. Unable to dramatize the evildoer, yet intimately acquainted with both the power of evil and the manifold shortcomings of the Jew, Jewish writers (and Jewish intellectuals) are always in danger of charging their fellow Jews for incurring the hatred against them.

Kafka, Babel, Proust had the artistic good fortune (perhaps combined with some personal misfortune) of being so thoroughly steeped in the native culture, including its anti-Semitic component, that they were able to portray a despiser of the Jews as well a Jew despised. Indeed, each of them went to dangerous, and possibly fatal, lengths to acquire this knowledge, which played such an important part in their writings. But Israeli Jews cannot be participants in Arab culture and they have no feeling for its interiority. They are unable to imagine the young boys who take out their penises to urinate on Israeli soldiers, let alone the mind of Yassir Arafat or George Habash and their trainees who spend their lives tracking Jews to kill. Israeli writers resemble instead those Yiddish and Hebrew writers of the diaspora whose languages confirmed their separateness from the surrounding culture, or those Holocaust survivors who could never really know their persecutors because they lived on the other side of a great moral divide. In itself, such limitation does not necessarily affect aesthetic achievement. No perspective is ever so narrow that it cannot yield great art, provided that it does not falsify. The danger of solipsism arises only when writers ascribe their own vision to others and mistake the reality of others for their own. Jewish writers and thinkers, in their eagerness to make the world as nice as they would like it to be, have been particularly prone to a solipsistic liberalism that has done great harm to both themselves and to the truth. It is sad to see so many Israeli writers returning to the internalization of the Jewish diaspora in their unequal struggle against Arab illiberalism. The rewards that they get from overseas readers and publishers for delivering up the image of the ugly Israeli cannot obscure the ugliness of the cultural trend that this image represents.

Chapter Seven

The Ultimate Test of Liberalism

At the beginning of August 1991 I attended a Seminar for Young European Jewish Leadership at a Komsomol Recreational Centre near Zvenigorod, about an hour and a half from Moscow. Three days after my departure, while the seminar was still in session, a state of emergency was imposed on the country by a junta of the Communist Party, and then events unfolded that marked the end of Communism for Russia, if not yet the dawn of an improved age. That gathering of young European Jews during the dying days of the Soviet Union assumed more than ordinary significance, for it was the first time since 1917 that Jews from all over the world had come together freely in Russia to celebrate and investigate their Jewishness, and it may have been the first time that Communist property had been made available to an independent international group. Since most of our sessions took place in a small hall under the obligatory red banner with the words "Long live the friendship of the people of the Soviet Union and the indestructible brotherhood of nations," it was impossible not to savor the sweet irony of historical reversal confirmed by the presence in that hall of our indestructible brotherhood of Jews.

On the eve of my departure for Russia, one of my colleagues at McGill had told me about his 1977 trip to the Soviet Union, when he spoke to a roomful of Jews about his field of specialization, the Hebrew Bible. After a scholarly presentation to people many of whom were themselves professionals and scholars in other areas, he was surprised by the first question, "Did the Exodus really happen?" He was even more surprised to hear himself respond, "You are the proof that it did." The supernatural improbability of the biblical story, which had embarrassed modern Jews from the moment of their enlightenment, now seemed to be the prooftext for the unfolding reality of their lives. While the downfall of Russian Communism is of profound significance to everyone in the world and of transforming importance to all the other religious and ethnic minorities that composed the Soviet Union, for the Jews it is as critically important as the defeat of German Nazism in 1945, virtually an opportunity of life over death. Since the tight political union that was forged between the Arab and Communist blocs between 1967 and 1990 had as its strongest bond military opposition to the Jewish state, defeat of Communism was a necessary precondition for eventual Arab reconciliation with Israel. Also, the suppression of Jewishness within the Soviet Union had made it prison-house to millions who would otherwise have left the country or else attempted to live there openly as Jews. No wonder, then, that the exodus of Jews from the Soviet Union and the signs of renewed Jewish life in Russia inspired even hardened rationalists to speak of miracles.

The collapse of the Soviet Union is an occasion for universal hope. But history teaches that momentous opportunities are seldom realized. Although Communism has failed, there is no guarantee that democracy will flourish in its stead, and although there is buoyant talk in some political circles of a "new world order," no satisfactory blueprints for this reorganization have yet surfaced. Great turning points are especially dangerous for the Jews, because in the uncertainty of change on a vast scale lies the still potent political option of blaming Jews for whatever retards the march of progress.

From this perspective, the fall of Communism may simply have turned back the clock to the beginning of the twentieth century. Recently liberated nations of the Communist bloc and slowly evolving nations of the Arab world are utterly unprepared for the competitive strains of modernity, and the populations of both these regions are accustomed to finding in the Jew the explanation for their woes. Will democratic and liberal polities and their leaders in Europe and North America stand up to the politics of anti-Semitism, or will they once again accommodate aggressors by sacrificing the Jews? Will the Jews, now with a country of their own, remain determined to achieve an unexceptional political status among the proliferating nations of the world, or will they quit the struggle in demoralizing numbers?

Russia was a good place to begin asking these questions.

The legacy of Communism, as I encountered it during my first visit, was shocking beyond anything I had imagined. Prepared by television reportage and the stories of Russian emigres for inefficiency and poverty on a very large scale, I was stunned by the enormity of devastation. It was as though everything that might have worked in this naturally beautiful country, every known form of association from the family to the political party, every human construction from private home to giant factory, had been deliberately deformed to ensure the misery of the inhabitants. The van that took us from the airport to our destination broke down (as it had on the trip to the airport), joining the chain of stranded vehicles along the road. The first gas station we passed was closed. From the second stretched two long lines, inert gray ribbons of men and machines. There were no places to snack or to eat, and except for a few brand-new English billboards advertising the *Reader's Digest* and *Business in the USSR*, no individuating, brightening colors on cars or landmarks. Yet neither was this a serene country of unexploited natural charm.

Whereas in certain other countries of Eastern Europe one has the feeling that improved management and imported resources might soon raise the standard of living, the anti-human central planning of the past seventy-five years in the Soviet Union destroyed every kind of infrastructure, except, perhaps, in villages that were left untouched. It seemed obvious to me that meaningful assistance could not even come from outside the country, since in the absence of indigenous units of production and distribution to absorb the imports and to begin reconstruction, the donations of

The Ultimate Test of Liberalism

well-meaning benefactors would only batten new tyrants, or else seep into waste. Using telephones that did not connect, in stores that sold nothing one would buy, among people who stood in line for basic commodities, I kept repeating to myself the words of the revolutionaries Chernyshevsky and Lenin: *"Chto Delat?"* (What Is To Be Done?) Their once rhetorical question now resounded with hopelessness.

In the condition of Jewish culture one could see how much the Communist regime had actually destroyed. The "Moscow Jewish Cultural and Educational Society" (sic) is the private creation of Yuri Socol, a decorated veteran of the Red Army. His apartment is on the ninth floor of a building with an elevator that holds four people. Of its two main rooms, one has been turned into a makeshift Jewish lending library, the second into a "museum of the Holocaust." We were told that this museum, which displays a few photographs and a few dozen English-language books, was the first of its kind, the first crack in the wall of official silence around the wartime destruction of the Jews.

Earlier in the century, this same city of Moscow had loomed as one of the centers of Jewish cultural creativity. Exceptionally gifted poets, writers, dramatists, journalists, and critics vied to contribute their talents to the new society. In the 1920s, the revolutionary atmosphere was sufficiently vibrant to attract many gifted Jewish emigres back from Western Europe and America to their native Russia. By the time they realized through what methods egalitarianism was to be achieved, the gates of the country had closed behind them. Then they tried to tailor their optimism to the narrowing opportunities for creative expression. As late as

If I Am Not For Myself

1948, despite the ubiquity of informers, the Yiddish intelligentsia continued to write, produce plays, edit critical volumes. Ironically, the war against Nazism allowed Jewish writers to speak out against the enemy, and once having rediscovered their voices as Jews, they found it hard to keep silent. Try as they might, they could not deny the Jewishness that flowed through their work like the blood through their veins, until Stalin put a stop to both by sentencing them to death.

Today the situation is reversed. Much as they want to express their Jewishness, the people coming to the makeshift library in Moscow, like virtually all the Jews remaining in Russia, have been stripped of culture as crudely as mines were once stripped of their ore. What is left, in some of the older Jews, seems less than nothing—mangled phrases of Yiddish, a few stale ideas filtered through Communist propaganda, the superstitious dregs of a magnificent religious tradition. Of course, it took great courage to establish a center of Jewish culture while such private initiative was still forbidden, and the young native Russian guides who described to us various local attempts to regenerate a Jewish life were visibly moved by the energy of self-taught Hebrew teachers, community leaders, fledgling rabbis, and by the founders of the library who had turned their private home into a public resource. Yet the effort and sacrifice of these people only accentuates how much had been lost. In place of a Russian Jewry that had once boasted of being the conscience of the Jews, a cluster of Jewish illiterates was now struggling over the Hebrew alephbet. It was almost too sad to be true.

The ruin of Jewishness under Communism was as complete as the ruin of Russia itself, but here emerges an apparent paradox. Communism and Zionism, two opposing ideological movements, had arisen at approximately the same time in modern history. Communism imposed its egalitarian, internationalist rule on Russia in the name of an improved humankind. The various Zionist parties, sometimes acting in concert and sometimes not, consolidated a place of refuge for the Jewish people. Communism was credited, even by some of its opponents, for its noble ideals, while Zionism was denounced, even by some whom it rescued, as a reactionary movement of narrow tribal interest.

As it turned out, Israel became the hospitable port of entry for fleeing victims of Communist repression, and many non-Jewish relatives of Soviet Jews clamored for exit visas to the Jewish state. Whereas Communism shaped a society indescribably humiliating and mean, Zionism gave birth to the most generous and one of the freest countries on earth. To fly from Moscow, where Lenin is entombed, to Jerusalem, where Herzl lies buried, is to see in brilliant clarity the lopsided verdict of history on the debates that rocked so many Jewish circles at the start of this revolutionary century. Moses Hess had foreseen this inversion of aims and ends in his critique of Marxism and his formulation of the Zionist idea. Jewish "parochialism" is always implicitly universal, since Jewish law recognizes both the legitimate existence of other peoples and the right of everyone who genuinely desires it to become a Jew. By contrast, universalist idealism in religion and politics is always implicitly repressive, since it expects everyone to become its particular species of universalist.

Furthermore, because the Jewish religious tradition translates ideals of holiness into practical, familial obligations, it has elevated *pidyon shevuyim*, the redemption of captives, into one of its highest precepts. Jews around the world felt duty-bound to rescue those who wanted to leave Russia, and for twenty years the Movement for Soviet Jewry fulfilled that duty, knowing that it could guarantee a port of entry for everyone it helped to free. Nor was Jewish assistance limited to potential emigres. Dozens of schools, seminars, summer camps, relief efforts, resource centers, have been established in Eastern Europe by American Jews and Israelis to bring knowledge and encouragement to both the staying and the leaving—who used to be known in Jewish politics at the beginning of the century by the Yiddish terms *do'istn* and *dortistn*—and if the remembered fate of the stayers-in-Europe in the first half of the century lends urgency to the policy of emigration, Israel offers repatriation, but no one can insist on it. Corresponding to the Jewish sense of responsibility that requires Jews to be their brothers' keepers is the absence of any central authority in Jewish life with the power to determine how those brothers are to live. Thus, while the manifest anti-Semitism of some Slavic nationalists prompted emergency evacuation to Israel of everyone who wished to flee, the new sprouting of Jewish culture in Europe demonstrates just how stubbornly Jews might be willing to hang on through centuries of persecution. For better or worse, the fractious and democratic Jews are too individual to be herded to any single destination, and too accustomed to wandering to become a homebound people overnight. This will ensure that Jews remain for the foreseeable future the barometer

The Ultimate Test of Liberalism

of tolerance, for no despot or despotism can tolerate a people, however small in numbers, that is at once so cosmopolitan in its instincts and so tribal in its obligations, so politically vulnerable and so ultimately indissoluble.

It is already obvious that the first and possibly the most serious consequence of the collapse of the Soviet empire will be gigantic population shifts of liberated peoples to more developed parts of the world. One stream of this tidal wave are the Russian Jews moving to Israel, who constitute the largest Jewish migration since the mass immigration to America at turn of the century. Like their predecessors, these Russian Jews may experience the satisfaction of contributing to the development of a young country, while enjoying all the opportunities of a democratic polity and a relatively open economy. Their arrival infuses Israel with new energy and confirms its moral achievement, no small matter for a nation of moral hypochondriacs. Their arrival also counteracts the efforts of the Arabs to undo the Jewish country by adding numbers to the citizenry and confidence to their self-image. But however welcome, the absorption of such a large and foreign group is accompanied by unpredictable problems. It is impossible to know in advance how an economy will react to the sudden outlay of money that is required for new housing and services, or how people without previous experience in democracy will adjust to existing democratic structures. What will be the consequence to a Jewish state of Jewish immigrants raised in totalitarian atheism who lack even vestigial memories of Sabbath, a Jewish holiday, a word of prayer? One wants to know—one has to know—whether

Communism has done irreparable damage to the capacity of human beings for cooperative competition, or if not, how long it will take for the damage to heal?

In December 1945, in a displaced persons camp near Munich, a group of Jewish survivors began putting out a weekly newspaper (in Yiddish with German script) called *Bamidbar* "*In the desert*, where we will not linger . . . on the way to our destination, Eretz Yisrael." The editors instinctively identified with the Israelite slaves who had been rescued by God and Moses from Egyptian bondage, sensing, perhaps, that despite their determination to move to Palestine and to make a new life for themselves, they would remain spiritually, if not physically, the desert generation of transition. One traditional explanation for the forty years of wandering that the Children of Israel had to endure—through the desert that could have been traversed in a matter of months—was the need to wait until the generation of slaves had died out so that a new self-disciplining generation born in freedom should begin the task of rebuilding Zion. At the Seminar for European Leadership I had just attended, a young woman from Oslo unconsciously took up the theme of *Bamidbar*, insisting that the forty years of post-war wandering through the desert were finally over, and that European Jews like herself felt healthfully free at last to take up creative Jewish national life, whether in Israel or in blood-stained Europe.

This image of the generation of the desert bears on the spiritual condition of Russian Jews coming to Israel and of the other refugees from Communist slavery. Slavery, after all, is not a propagandistic barb of Cold War politics, and not a description of those who served time in the Gulag, but the accurate term for people whose knowledge, beliefs, education, expression, professional ambition, income, habitation, mobility, and recreation were dictated by the state. As no one can know how long it will take for people born and raised under government oppression to adapt to the frightening opportunity of freedom, it helps to keep in mind the biblical minimum of forty years and to consider what has to be done to develop in newly released captives the capacities for responsible liberty. The first thing to be done is to rehearse the distinction between the two conditions. Freedom, which requires perpetual rededication to onerous responsibilities, can only be sustained by a population that knowingly and repeatedly rejects its seductive alternative.

The collapse of Communism is very different from the defeat of Nazism almost half a century earlier. The ideology of Nazism was so thoroughly embodied in the power of the Nazi state that it took no more than the defeat of the state to demolish the idea upon which it had been based. In sharpest contrast, the Communist ideal was forged by intellectuals, who far from speaking in the name of power, pretended to be mere instruments of historical determinism and of a benevolent progressivism that would bring about a perfected society. So firm was the ideological association of Communism with idealism that even today vast segments of the liberal community are prepared to separate the repressive policies of all actual Communist governments from the perfection of those that may yet exist in the future, perpetuating the ideal of the egalitarian state that proved so dangerous in the first place. We note that liberal opinion expresses no belated gratitude to Ronald Reagan for having opposed the "evil empire" and experiences no crisis of conscience for having failed to do the same. Far from ensuring the spread of democracy as the superior alternative to the controlling state, the dissolution of the Soviet Union does not even appear to have had the effect of reinforcing an appreciation of democracy where it already exists. Without moral reckoning—in politics as in personal life—there can be no moral improvement; yet there is still no widespread recognition in the liberal community that any such self-scrutiny might be in order.

One of the great strengths of Jewish civilization is its insistence on keeping alive the memory of its own past misdeeds and errors as a means of ensuring at least some civilizing improvement. Moral self-scrutiny is undertaken in a spirit different from that of the legal system, for the penitent seeks to improve himself without waiting to be nabbed by others. Liberal democracy, too, would have to know and remember and teach its children about the temptation of Communism were it really concerned with political morality and personal goodness. Why, in particular, did the liberal community in North America continue to waltz to what the American writer Vivian Gornick called "the Romance of Communism" long after the music had choked on the blood of sixty million of its own subjects? Why was the suffering of leftists under McCarthyism used to obscure the horrors of Stalinism, and why did "Reds" remain the heroes of Hollywood with no thought for the suffering of their victims? Since Jews have always boasted of their prominence in the liberal-left, they cannot be exempted from this judgment, and since the Jewish Left in particular has always boasted of its morality, it owes itself some hard examination.

The Ultimate Test of Liberalism

This is the most painful of all the issues we have raised so far, and given what one knows of the adversaries of the Jews, also the most dangerous. Consider this analogy: Suppose a dozen or more gangsters have committed a major crime—the boss who planned it, the gunmen who murdered innocent bystanders, the safecrackers and thieves who executed the robbery, the lookouts, the getaway drivers, the fences who laundered the money. Of them all, only one develops a conscience when they are finally caught and brought to trial. Suppose, further, that the one with the conscience had been pegged all along by the others as the fall guy—precisely because of his predisposition to self-reproach and moral scruple. When, after they have all been apprehended, the other members of the gang try to pin their crime on this designated scapegoat, should he cooperate with them in assuming any part of the blame? In addition to making himself their victim, would not his penchant for confession pervert the system of justice by helping to exonerate the other criminals, and even worse, would he not ensure the spread of crime by letting them off scot-free?

Anti-Semitism in Eastern Europe justifies itself today through the association of Jews with Communism. Knowing how tempted many Russians, Poles, Ukrainians, Lithuanians, and others are to escape the hardest part of reconstruction by doing what they habitually have done, blaming the Jews for their mistakes and wrongdoings (even, when as in Poland, there are almost no Jews left to blame), one is almost afraid to discuss the involvement of a minority of Jews with Communism, and the false hopes that it stirred in many others. Since the ratio of self-reproach to self-congratulation is exceedingly high in Jews, other peoples have learned to exploit this scrupulousness to their advantage, inviting the Jewish specialists-in-guilt to do penance for everyone's crimes. One would not want to assist them in such self-deception. Earlier I argued against the tendency of Jews to assume blame for crimes committed by others, and I would appear to be contradicting myself by suggesting that they apologize for the regimes that oppressed them and sought their dissolution as a people.

So let me make it absolutely clear that Jews owe no one else an accounting. Communist rulers of Communist regimes and Communist functionaries who carried out immoral orders stand in the same relation to their subject peoples as the rulers and functionaries of Nazi Europe, guilty of crimes they committed under the law, of having exempted themselves from the reach of the law, and of having distorted the law to protect some citizens at the expense of others. Because Russia will not be prosecuted for its crimes by any international tribunal, it will have to perform its own moral autopsy to determine the harm that it did to its own people and to the countries it conquered. In the same way, in every democratic country, leftist fellow travelers who assisted and liberals who did nothing to retard the spread of Communism have to examine their consciences, just as they expect Nazi sympathizers to do.

Nonetheless, while refusing to take the rap for a system they did not control, Jews are obliged to account for themselves, and in the modern period this means knowing why and how, as a rule of thumb, the temptation to political sin comes to them from the Left rather than the Right.

The Ultimate Test of Liberalism

Distinguished from Christians and Muslims by their refusal to believe that a messiah or messianic prophet has already come, Jews have not attempted to win other peoples over to their vision of redemption and have thus avoided the temptations of political power. But being, as they were, at the mercy of other peoples, their corresponding temptation was making a virtue of powerlessness. Many times during the past 2,500 years, Jewish sects abandoned Jewish teachings and embraced a newly declared messiah in an attempt to reverse their earthly misfortune, just as in the modern period of declining religious faith, secular ideological movements hoped to transcend the Jewish condition through a radical transformation of society that would make Jews obsolete.

Rabbinic tradition always warned against hastening the end of history, for it understood that unleashed idealism could interrupt the incremental improvement of mankind that Jewish law was trying to effect. The rabbis tried to maintain equilibrium between conservative ritual and prophetic impatience so that, for example, if the Torah reading for the Day of Atonement is the finicky description of penitential sacrifice from Leviticus 16, it is followed immediately by the Haftorah reading from Isaiah that scoffs at mere ritual and insists on its ethical substance. Steering the difficult course between a potentially stultifying legalism and the complementary danger of idealism trying to break free of the human condition, the rabbis found it hardest to maintain a balanced civilization in periods of great promise or threat. To Rabbi Yokhanan ben Zakkai, first-century leader of the Pharisees, is attributed the teaching: If there be a plant in your hand when they say to you, "Behold the Messiah!" first go to plant the plant, and afterward go out to greet him. One can sense in this warning how powerfully the redemptive promise must have tempted Jews under Roman rule to forfeit their constraining Jewish way of life to the hope of being freed of it.

When, many centuries later, a similar climate of oppression made modern European Jews susceptible to political faiths of messianic intensity, a great many Jews stopped "planting their plants," stopped cultivating their own garden, and went out to join the redemptive movements. Abraham Cahan, long-time editor of the *Jewish Daily Forward* declared socialism to be the new Torah of the Jews and tried to transpose the moral core of Judaism, now freed as in Christianity from its husk of the Law, into a new secular faith. Yet without the nay-saying and restricting accumulations of habit that the rabbis had established as the basis of a sound way of life, and without the assumption of full responsibility for the national family, Jewishness dribbled away into irrelevance or into compulsive optimism. Were modern Jews now to engage in the kind of acute soul-searching that Jewish religious practice encourages, they would have to confess not, as they falsely do, for Arab crimes against them but for the consequences of their "idealism," for their readiness to sacrifice their fellow Jews to the ambitions of other peoples, for their slowness in reclaiming full political autonomy in Zion, and for their failure to bring to its fullest potential the Jewish civilization into which they were born.

All the while, freedom in history is represented by those

The Ultimate Test of Liberalism

Jews who continue to maintain a disciplined Jewish way of life and a responsible Jewish community. It was Jewish nationalism rather than Jewish socialism that proved the more powerful force of liberation in this century, creating the first democratic state in the Middle East, weakening Communism internally through Jewish dissent, and thwarting the expansion of Communism through Israel's repeated defeat of Soviet client states. Since some of the most tyrannical rulers of the twentieth century considered the Jews the supreme danger to their hegemony, whoever stood up for the Jews stood up against Czarism and Communism, against Hitler and Stalin and Saddam Hussein, for individual rights and democratic freedoms, and international justice. In fact, the level of commitment to democratic freedom and individual rights in any group or society can probably be tested most effectively by the single indicator of its readiness to protect the rights of the Jews. (Protection of other minorities will not test tolerance in the same way, because other minorities often join in discriminating against the Jews.) Whereas ideological internationalism, which sought the dissolution of the Jews as the first step toward an undifferentiated humanity, invested its good intentions in projects that were at best quixotic, at worst murderous, the defense of the Jews remained the surest test of liberal values.

The world as I write is so politically changeable that cartography assumes the properties of a lottery. Europe is no longer divided between east and west; the Cold War coalitions have been revised; Japan and China rather than the United States and the Soviet Union now represent the poles of capitalism and communism; African history will hence-forth be determined by warring blacks; the balance of power in the Middle East keeps shifting between autocratic sheiks, demagogic strong men, and religious fundamentalists. Inundated by the news of man-made disasters from all parts of the globe, we feel almost justified in withdrawing from the political arena with a shrug of resignation, and sending off a couple of checks to foreign rescue operations to absolve our aching sense of impotence.

As part of the international confusion, we note also the increasing prominence of Jew-blame, not only in the Middle East where it is a standard feature of political indoctrination, but—for reasons this book tries to explain—even in American politics, from which it had almost disappeared. Because blame of the Jews will emerge as one of the few common elements of the Left and the Right, because blame of the Jews exacts almost no political price, and because blame of the Jews is so much easier than standing up to the aggression against them, more and more people will be tempted to abandon the Jews to their fate, or to respond that they "do not know" which side is in the right.

Many Jews, too, will want to leave politics behind or otherwise disengage themselves from an unpopular cause. Since politics is in any case an unwelcome intruder into nobler spiritual and intellectual pursuits, they may retire to their inner life—to prayer and study as in days of yore, or to debates over religion and culture, diaspora and Israel, particularism and universalism, socialism and capitalism. Their geniuses will spin out universalist theories of poetics and

The Ultimate Test of Liberalism

economics and grammar and physics, while their political debaters will become increasingly ghettoized, instead of taking their argument out to the public. The one subject Jews will least want to address is the condition that keeps them in the international limelight by refusing them the right to an unexceptional existence. While the Arabs try to escape their social and economic problems by projecting blame and responsibility onto the Jews and expend their creative energies in trying to eliminate the Jewish presence, the Jews increasingly do the same, but in reverse. They waste their creative energies trying to eliminate the Arab presence— from their minds.

For all that has changed in world affairs, the fate of Jews in the last half of the twentieth century depends on the Arabs to the same degree that the fate of Jews in the 1930s depended on the Germans, and it remains to be seen how the other nations will react to the outrage of anti-Jewish politics this time around. The unimaginable has already happened many times over—as when the president of the United Nations General Assembly, a Saudi Arabian, walked out of the Assembly, which he was expected to chair impartially, because *as an Arab* he refused to be present during the speech of the representative of Israel! By sitting calmly through it all, representatives of the democratic nations gave Arabs the signal in the precise language of diplomacy that the Jews may be as expendable to the family of nations as the Arabs consider them to be. No other nation would have been shown the same contempt.

Despite the indignity of their political situation, Jews

cannot be excused from facing it, for only if they stand up to Arab enmity can they claim to be maintaining human rights. Jews will never prove themselves moral by seeking refuge from their struggle behind the banner of liberalism. But liberalism assuredly will be judged by whether it can protect the Jews.

Reflections on Love and Loyalty

Dear B,

This is about as far away from you as I will ever be. I'm at the cottage on the lake, deserted now at the beginning of September by all but the heartiest of the summer people. I came out here to close the place while the rest of the family continued southward to New York. Once I'd stripped the beds and polished the kitchen and vacuumed the floors and scoured the toilets, I felt I deserved a swim so I put on a bathing suit and went down to the lake in the hour that Hebrew calls "between the suns." A chipmunk scampered out of my way down the stairs and under the porch. An unseasonal fly brushed my arm as I crossed the grass to the dock. After that everything was so still that no matter how smooth I tried to make my strokes they sliced the water like a defilement. I swam for what seemed a very long time when, suddenly, I heard the love-sick trilling of a loon on the other side of the bay. That loon's cry is making me wild.

Normally the loon utters a long call, like a small shofar on the high holidays. I listen to it sometimes in the middle of the night, wondering how a solitary sound can be so soothing. I imagine the trees, black silhouettes, framing the water, the moon barely visible from behind the clouds, and that motionless, elegant bird illumined in a peacefulness as rich as Eden's. If I can persuade myself that I am similarly suspended on the cool water among the tall trees, I fall back into a calm sleep.

The loons around here have grown quite tame. When we first began coming to the Adirondacks I thought they were extinct, only their images preserved on regional postcards and door-stoppers. Nowadays, it looks as though the Park Commission has won at least part of its battle for the preservation of the environment. When you row out on the lake a loon may approach to within an oar's length of the boat and wait there to be admired. They don't seem to mind intrusions on even their deepest privacy. This late in the year, I don't suppose that could be the cry of their mating out there in the bay, but still its vibration stirs the blood.

Stirs my blood. As at that other shore at Dahab when we uttered small cries of our own. I haven't thought about that night for years (after years of thinking about that night) and I wasn't eager to be reminded of it, let alone out here among the horny loons. But now that the memory's pierced me, I'm crazy with restlessness like a teenager, may God help me. I try so hard to discipline my wayward desires (quack, quack) wear what the children call teacher's shoes, let hair turn gray to

Epilogue: Reflections on Love and Loyalty

give proofs of aging flesh (quack, quack) walk miles a day, play sweaty tennis, do many good deeds to tame the beast (quack, quack), and I am really middle-aged besides. That quacking, incidentally, is no invention of mine but of Saul Bellow, a man who never does stop quacking, whatever the cost to him in alimony or peace of mind. When in one of his books I first came upon this aging man's mockery of his ageless man's desire I laughed, as a young woman does who imagines the bird in pursuit of herself. But by now the laughter has died. A graying man may make fun of himself because he can either succeed or fail in his friskier pursuits. A graying woman doesn't even have the option of playing the fool.

I've never understood how I could have spent the first day in your presence without noticing you. Let me say in self-defense that the scene greeting me at the parking lot when I turned up there at 6 A.M. was so different from what I had expected that it took me quite a while to get my bearings. Believe it or not, I had looked forward to solitude. My husband was holed up in a Jerusalem legal office with the battling parties who were paying his bills, and instead of the two days he thought his deal would take to straighten out, he said he would be lucky to have things cleared up by the time we were scheduled to return to Montreal. For some reason, this hurtled me down a chute of self-pity. I had arranged for baby-sitters back home, planned two weeks of meals and schedules so that I could take this "well-deserved holiday" with my husband, and there I was at the end of autumn, with a full year of teaching awaiting me at home, and without the excursion I had been promised. So I decided to take one on my own. I thought of traveling through the Galilee, but the Hofsteins recommended one of the Sinai trips that they had taken over Passover, and that's how I got the idea of six days in the desert. Their descriptions were all of the sand and the sea; the only human aspect they mentioned was the store-house of bones of the deceased monks at the monastery of Santa Katherina. About the climb up Mount Sinai that was advertised as the climax of the trip they said nothing, though they did allow that I might be interested in seeing where Jewish civilization was presumably fashioned. It never occurred to me until I actually showed up at dawn with my borrowed sleeping bag and canteen and saw the two open trucks filling up with people that this was not going to be a solitary adventure but an extended overnight camping trip, the sort of thing that in my countless seasons at summer camp I would have gone to any lengths to avoid.

What a disaster! Again, I had been robbed of the promised holiday, only this time I had no one to blame but myself and my lack of imagination. The worst moment was when one of the guides invited all the English speakers to get into one of the trucks and all French speakers into the other; and because the French speakers were in the minority, would those of us who understood French be good enough to join the second group so that we could travel with our appropriate guide. Oh God! A guide! Lectures on the habits of the Bedouin and on the hieroglyphics of the ancient Habiru! And in French! Because of course on holiday or not and no matter how choked with dismay I would never pass up an appeal to my civic duty. Before the outsized jeep even turned a wheel, I had given up any hope of pleasure.

Epilogue: Reflections on Love and Loyalty

I suppose that's the best way to set out on any venture—drained of hope, dumb, sore, miserable. I found myself an outside seat in back where the sand dust soon began to transform me into a caked desert creature. For a couple of hours the only use I made of my mouth was to sip regularly from the canteen as we had been told to do. By the time we stopped at our first watering hole—that shack along the road with an outhouse in back and something frying on a hot plate in the broiling sun—my spirits had begun to improve. The parched texture of my hair and jeans and the inside of my throat reassured me that civilization was being left behind.

And naturally, no sooner did it begin to be satisfied than my craving for solitude yielded to curiosity. In front of me sat the pair of kibbutz girls who were given the trip as a treat between high school and the army. This much I made out from their fumbling conversation with the chatterbox who sat beside them (thankfully, not beside me). The girl directly in front of me had a rosy neck with a marvellously thick black braid, while the one on the inside was blond and tanned, as though she had already spent the summer on army maneuvers. What made me notice the dark one especially was the way she kept stealing a look at our driver-guide, Dudu. If you recall, he stopped the car once on a rise above Jericho to tell us something about the city, and he could claim a girl's interest, no doubt of that. He was short, muscular, and bronze, and as I had watched him take off his jeans before he got into the driver's seat I knew there was no line either at the belly or the thigh of his bathing trunks to indicate a more natural color of skin. I linger on the physique because there wasn't much in his brief talk to compete with it for attention.

Black Braid in front of me seemed to have been smitten on the spot, and I thought that the fantasy she would spin out for the next few days would probably constitute her first real brush with love.

Still, at that point I wasn't really looking around. I did learn that the chatterbox was a lapsed nun from a convent in Switzerland. When Dudu prodded us to take periodic drinks of water she offered me her canteen, but I declined so as not to have to engage in the conversation she seemed desperate to initiate. Behind me were the Italian father and son and beside them the two French fellows making a play for Janie, the sophomore from Harvard. I heard a French-Canadian accent that later turned out to belong to the teacher from Trois Rivières. The pair beside me, the honeymooners, slept. Do you remember any of this?

It was when we picked up those two couples in Eilat that you first caught my eye. I wish I could say it was you that I noticed—what I noticed was your reaction to them. Had this been a movie, the music would have soared then, along with your expressive eyebrow, marking the onset of The Plot. Even today, at a remove of twenty years, I see those four people coming towards us from the hotel, so utterly implausible that either they or we would have had to be embarrassed by our encounter—and they, like royalty, were not the ones to be embarrassed. The men were strictly accompaniment: two studs in aviator glasses with gold trim that matched the white and gold pattern of their shirts. They looked as if they had been making for the ocean and had stumbled inland by mistake. The woman on the arm of the stouter, rough-looking man was the most beautiful I had ever seen, her hair

Epilogue: Reflections on Love and Loyalty

that cascade of yellow and gold that is featured in commercials for the most expensive shampoos. Her face was perfectly serene, like the surface of the lake here in front of me or a baby's smile after nursing. Her skin was honey, and so much of it in view! She was wearing iridescent blue and silver satin shorts in a style I saw featured in *Vogue* the following summer and a halter of white satin. Its contents would have seemed as satisfactory as all the rest of her had it not been for the woman beside her, dressed almost identically, but with large softly bobbing breasts that every male hand must have been itching to steady. This dark lady had a hilly nose and pockmarked skin, but no pity was to be wasted on the homely one who walked in the shadow of the beauty. Her breasts and the vitality that kept them in motion sent out a challenge of their own: that one's made for the canvas, but I'm for the sheet. And as though to complete the symmetry, hers was the handsomer of the two men.

What kept the breasts bobbing, then and for the rest of the trip, were the three-inch heels of her sandals. At the sight of those preposterous heels our guides should have administered a brief lecture on the requirements of desert travel, promised a refund, and turned the foursome back. Hadn't the information leaflet specified good walking shoes as the most important item of our attire? Sensible dress—for the kind of journey that the children of Israel had taken forty years to complete, and for the climb up the mountain where Moses was said to have conversed with God. Those heels were a breach of contract, an insult to us and to the desert. I suppose that they were also the sign of royalty, which advertises its contempt for commoners. The contempt of these imperious strangers for our well-behaved little group issued from the soles of their feet rather than from the regal crown of the head, but it had the similar effect of subduing us all. Our trained desert guides could no more have contravened their wishes than we could take our eyes off them. Obligingly, the guides loaded up the Gucci luggage into the back of the truck, and helped those bimbos up the steps!

I was incensed, but you were amused. You must have recognized that any man with a bone in his body would have done the same. That's exactly what you said to me hours later when we were leaving the campfire. "You can't really blame the guides. Any man with a bone in his body would have done the same." How could I help falling in love with you?

There's time now—what else but time, now?—to ask you all the questions I didn't ask then, such as, what made you want me? how soon were you sure you had me? how much did you enjoy me? To tell the truth, though, the sexual reassurance I once wanted from you through this line of questioning has either been satisfied or else it has dissipated, and my curiosity turns philosophical with age. Right now I'm wondering whether we would have acted so precipitously had those sensualists not joined our company, and had we not been obliged to sit as involuntary witnesses in the rows behind them all that long first afternoon. The sight of them tossing cigarette butts and then the empty cigarette packs over the side of the truck in defiance of the guides' explicit instructions and the ex-nun's tearful plea not to "torture the desert"—didn't that undermine our respect for the rules? Or Martine washing her painted toenails—her toenails!—with the water we had been told was as precious as diamonds? And when they caressed one another with fingertips and eyes, weren't they provoking our envy and taunting us for our modesty—and didn't they succeed? Understand, I'm not looking for an excuse here. Quite the contrary. Our adultery would be shameful as well as sinful if I knew that it had been inspired by barbarians. I'm only wondering whether the behavior of those four people didn't goad us into shedding some of the burden of civilization that we had brought on the trip along with our solid walking shoes?

That first night, for example. Suppose that after supper the guides had gathered us around the campfire for the obligatory evening program and asked us to make our introductions: Hello, I am Anna from Indiana. Marie from Paree. Chaim from Yerushalayim. Nediv from Tel Aviv. We would have sat there, you and I, as dutifully as we had been following orders all day. We would have joined in the singing of "Hava Nagila" and "Everybody Loves Saturday Night," not merely complying with our group leaders but as former camp counselors ourselves, solicitous of their attempt to create the illusion of community among us strangers. We would have shown esprit de corps (meaning the body collective rather than the body private). Finally, damped like the fire by so much induced enthusiasm, we would have gone to our separate sleeping bags under the stars. "Good night," we would have said to one another, or maybe *"Layla tov.* See you tomorrow."

But the guides had been intimidated. When the Frenchmen refused to do their assigned clean-up detail after supper, the guides fell back on a strategy of self-defense. The tall one—Tsvi?—improvised neatly and pretended that he had issued them an invitation to join evening activity rather than an order to do their rotation. But he must have known that he was forfeiting his authority, even as he feigned indifference to it. The guides stuffed the potatoes back into the supply bags. They doused the fire and sent us off to bed without song or story. We were left to fend for ourselves. You came over to me then and as we walked in the direction of the sleeping bags, you said there was no point in blaming the guides— intimating that all men are the same when the blood begins to pound. I was very happy to take the cue.

I was not a sexual novice by the time we met. There had been in addition to many years of fruitful marriage some brightening dalliance on otherwise miserable Montreal midwinter afternoons. I was also a serious reader; from texts of the sexual revolution that was poisoning the atmosphere faster than acid rain I had been instructed that the real duty of a wife was not to her husband but to her genitalia. As part of that dubious teaching I had been told about my natural right to climax and orgasm and satisfaction, and also techniques for achieving that satisfaction. Out there in the desert it was beside the point. *Vilde khaye* my mother had shouted at me one day when as a teenager I went crashing in a rage around the kitchen, but she mistook my calculated rebellion against her for loss of control. With you I really did feel like a wild animal. I couldn't repossess my trembling body. I realized in myself the frightening properties of fire.

During the daytime we were very well behaved. We barely touched, as if to demarcate our moral and aesthetic distance from the French couples. Towards the end of the second day when as if by magic we came upon the shaded pool in the wadi and went in for a dip, our thighs happened to brush in

Epilogue: Reflections on Love and Loyalty

the water and we swam apart as if burned. Without confer-
ring, I think we both considered it a point of pride to remain
undiscovered for the duration of the trip. Maybe we even
worked harder to prove ourselves good citizens. In the
mornings I scoured the breakfast pans whether or not it was
my turn. You were the first to leap down when the truck
developed a flat, to help the guides change the tire. Gradually, you began to be entrusted with some of the unraveled
authority, and people came to you instead of to the guides
with their problems. The ex-nun wanted you to help arrange
some privacy for body functions; you suggested that whenever
we stopped for lunch or for supper the trucks be placed in a
certain formation and that an area beyond them be blocked
off for "toilets." The guides went along with your solution.
Having once yielded to semisavages, they could hardly object
to the demands of the hypercivilized. You and I were the
secret savages, swollen with pleasure at night, lean with
restraint by day.

Have you ever read *Tristan and Isolde*, that profoundly
un-Jewish love story? It ambushed me during my sophomore
year at college in a course on Romanticism. Tristan the loyal
servant is sent to bring back Isolde, the bride of his beloved
master King Mark, much as in chapter twenty-four of
Genesis the servant of Abraham is instructed to seek out and
bring back a bride for Isaac. But how different are the
complications in the gentile tale! The nurse who accompanies Isolde (quite unlike the careful nurse who accompanies
Rebecca) has taken along a magical love potion to be drunk
by the king and his queen at their wedding, thus ensuring
their abiding marital love. Before the destination is reached,

however, there is a huge storm at sea, during which Tristan and Isolde accidentally slake their thirst with that magical drink. There is no help for them thereafter. "And they gave themselves up utterly to love."

Utterly! This same act of unholy fornication that the biblical narrator is prepared to punish unto the tenth generation whenever it occurs (because its consequences can so easily work their way unto the tenth generation) the medieval gentile narrator exalts for its purity and glorifies for its beauty. He doesn't just bring these lovers together and shrug his shoulders at the fateful mistake, but he adores their sin. By having the trusted nurse proffer the cup of passion to them and during a storm when all normal caution is suspended, he absolves the lovers in advance for the adultery they will practice over a lifetime. He invites us to feel the marvellous absolutism of their passion. Isolde who betrays both men, her husband with her mind and her lover with her body, looms as the holy grail of Tristan's permanent quest. And Tristan—betrayer of the master to whom he pledged obedience—is treated by the narrative as an erotic Christ. These earthly lovers are as doomed as Jesus, paying with their martyrdom for an attachment of such intensity. Through the beauty of the text, the surrender of these lovers to absolute passion routs all earlier notions of marital fidelity.

Much has been written about the political and religious meaning of this idea of love in the Western world, but its heretical effect on me was unmediated by any knowledge of its history or source. Had I been asked to describe love prior to the reading of *Tristan and Isolde*, I would have invoked the sturdy affection of my mother and father who held hands when they came to visit me one summer at camp, and whose marriage, crowded with bills and intestinal maladies, was as flawed as ordinary life tends to be. Came the Tristan legend to teach that forbidden love was not only stronger but ever so much "holier" than the sanctified kind. Thanks to you, I had a chance to test that proposition.

Did I say earlier that the two French couples seemed regal in their contempt for the rest of us? Only at first. Their physical grace and glittering attire set them apart for a time, but they were too coarse to keep our interest for very long, and, in fact, once its novelty wore off their vulgarity was as predictable as the public propriety of small-town churchgoers. You and I, on the other hand, became increasingly inventive through our duplicity. We spoke a double-tiered language, our innocent public utterance spiked with provocative private allusions. Making camp, breaking camp, preparing food—everything that involved our hands and fingers pointed to the night of pleasure ahead of us, and whenever our eyes caught in the process, became part of an extended foreplay. Because we kept it hidden, our attraction to one another acquired mysterious intensity, and we were like members of a secret sect whose superiority battens on their pretended normalcy. We became conspirators as well as lovers, and how can ordinary experience, even "ordinary" love, compete with the excitement of subterfuge? Pricked by the danger of discovery, and hallowed by intervals of abstinence, we gave ourselves up utterly to love.

If I am not mistaken, something changed in the nature of the trip the day we climbed the mountain. By then, we had all grown accustomed to being ferried around by truck on a prearranged itinerary complete with "unexpected discoveries" of pools of rainwater in the wadis and ancient carvings on shielded rocks. Even our sudden encounter on day three with the small convoy of military jeeps among the sand dunes was probably no surprise to the guides, who must have been well briefed about everything that was going on in the area. Whatever little we did for ourselves, such as making the fire and cleaning up, we were called upon to do as part of an established routine, but it wasn't we who planned the meals or decided how far we should travel each day. Thus the shift from horizontal to vertical movement on the day we climbed Sinai would have occasioned a shift of attitude had it been only an anonymous mountain we were climbing. Once we left behind the well-stocked vehicles and set out on foot with our supplies on our backs, we reverted into the loose collection of individuals we had been originally, of varying sizes, shapes, levels of energy, spirit, and will. On foot, we resumed for the first time independent responsibility for our progress.

These adjustments might have gone very smoothly. By the standards of mountaineering, Sinai is an easy climb, no more than two hours or so for good hikers. Tsvi because he was the tallest guide would have stayed out in front, setting the pace, pointing out to the eager climbers around him certain landmarks or quirks of the path. The second guide would have sustained the middle of the group with anecdotes or songs, while Dudu held up the rear with encouraging praise and reassurances. That, at any rate, was how we started out, and the ease with which the guides set up the pattern suggests how often and effortlessly they had done it before.

Epilogue: Reflections on Love and Loyalty

Martine's sandals tripped them up. It began as a joke, her clattering up the mountain supported by her two *pieds noir* (as by then they had been identified) with the gorgeous Chantale giggling merrily alongside. Their foursome had been functioning as a group within the group in any case, rarely speaking to the rest of us except to complain to the guides, and there was a certain relief in putting them out of sight at our rear. But as the peals of merriment kept falling farther behind, the groups were in danger of splitting off from one another, and every time the guides tried to hold us back to keep those sounds within earshot, resentment at the front of the line grew bolder. Why had she been allowed to come on the climb in defiance of all sanity and safety? Why should we respect the needs of people who didn't know the meaning of respect? How could trained guides have sacrificed all of us to the whims of one spoiled brat? The sandal-metronome kept slowing us down, until it stopped altogether and then news traveled up the line that one of the lady's heels had broken off and gone tumbling down the rocks. A chorus wished its owner a similar fate.

My God, how the pent-up furies exploded then! Everyone seemed to be shouting at once, down the mountain at Martine and her companions, at the guides, at one another. The Italian father swore that if Tsvi did not proceed immediately with him and his son and whoever else was ready to advance, he himself would lead the group in spite of not knowing the way. The anger I had felt when they first joined our company in Eilat, eclipsed by stronger emotions during the intervening days, was now back in a flash, and I too wanted to defy the guides by setting out for the top of the mountain at the fastest possible clip. I noticed that even for the honeymooning pair the honeymoon was suspended. The bridegroom was hollering that he would report the guides to the tour company for having endangered the group, and the bride sulked unbecomingly.

As I recall, two people stayed calm. One was the lapsed nun from Switzerland who began to make her way down the mountain to where Martine was stranded in her damaged slippers, so that she might offer the distressed damsel the sturdy sandals off her own feet. Passing us on her way down she explained that with her hardened soles and greater experience as a climber, she could proceed barefoot, whereas Martine's handicap might force us all to abandon our project. When the plan was broached to Martine, she accepted of course, and pronounced the flat sandals not a bad fit. Pure egoists are the greatest beneficiaries of pure Christians. I was not as angry with Martine as I was with the nun, and there is no further point in referring to her as the "lapsed nun," because she was obviously still in the grip of the same self-abnegating idea that had impelled her to enter the convent.

I was angriest with the guides for permitting this travesty. They allowed the nun to atone for their gross error of judgment. Instead of protecting her equal right to enjoy the trip she had paid for, they sacrificed her convenience for their own. You may have felt similarly dissatisfied with their behavior, because with calm authority it was you who took over the leadership of the group from that point on. I don't know exactly what you said to the guides, but we were told to start moving ahead with you as our new anchor. Dudu would drop behind to oversee the Parisian foursome, now joined by the nun. If they ran into any more difficulties, he would summon help with his walkie-talkie, but otherwise they would proceed at their speed and we at ours. If they couldn't make it to the top, they would return to the prearranged rendezvous spot of the trucks where we would rejoin them eventually.

The day was well advanced by then, and the early start we had counted on to get a jump on the sun had been lost along with the broken heel. It grew hotter as we climbed. Despite the heat, we of the main group forced ourselves up the mountain at a very brisk pace, scampering up the rocks, pulling one another up over difficult spots in the path. Once or twice we were reminded to drink from our canteens, but otherwise no one said very much, neither the guides to explain nor we to inquire. At the narrowing top of the mountain we discovered, with a mixture of gratitude and annoyance, the carved steps into the stone and small railings of wood that previous travelers had provided at the steepest points in the path. Their welcome assistance was a less than welcome reminder that we were part of a relentless tourist stream and that those following us up the mountain, the likes of Martine and her companions, would in the years to come undoubtedly advocate a paved road or a chair lift for their greater convenience. Then, abruptly, these small disturbing thoughts were interrupted. We had heaved ourselves out on the plateau and arrived at our destination. A lyric from my teenage folksinging days came unbidden to memory, drowning out all the more exalted phrases of Scripture: "If I could I surely would / Stand on the rock where Moses stood." There we were indeed, standing in the footsteps of Moses.

The landscape that greets the eye up there could not have changed very much in the millenia since Moses' sojourn— hills of yellowing orange, some slightly higher and some slightly lower than the mountain designated as Sinai, stretching out to the horizon beyond. If sand and wind had caused some alteration in the shape and hues of the surrounding hills and valleys, they hadn't reduced the expanse of barrenness. The scene from where we stood was nowhere as stark as, say, Mount Washington above the tree line where you crawl over blackening rocks and feel the frightening aspect of the original primeval chaos—the biblical *"tohu vavohu."* I've never climbed the Himalayas or the Alps, those peaks that tempt ambitious human creatures to their glory or their doom. Sinai reminded me rather of the rabbinic commentary that asks how so unassuming a mountain was given the honor of so remarkable an event. The rabbis who knew of its relative size wondered why this undistinguished place had been granted such historical prominence. I suppose that when God granted human beings free will, he also granted it to the world they traveled. Moses conferred grandeur on the mountain, not the mountain on Moses. When the Law was given to those who agreed to be bound by it, its reception transformed that otherwise ordinary mound of sand and stone into a holy site.

You made a comment there that I've never forgotten: you said it was a strange place to have conceived the Law. At the time I was touched by your apparent identification with

Moses as a fellow "lawyer" and by the word "conceived" that left open all the questions of authorship. Your metaphor cleverly credited Moses with having borne the Torah through its long period of gestation without specifying the impulse, divine or human, of its conception. Thinking about your comment now, I'm struck by another aspect altogether, not the who but the what of the conception. That mountaintop in the desert was certainly a strange place to have conceived the *Law*. Isn't that what you meant?

Moses was the leader-guide of a rabble of former slaves crossing the desert on their way back from Egypt to their own land, Eretz Yisrael. At a certain point on this arduous journey, he abandoned his quarreling charges and retired for forty days to the top of this mountain. Why else retire from the encumbrance of slaves but to burst free of them into a purer air? Solitary at last, an audience of one, he would have registered every item of God's repertoire—each glint and echo, spoor of life, crumble of sandstone. Sun-scorched, he might have entertained visions of angels floating down from the heavenly cloudbeds to fan his brow. From Moses on the mountain, one would have expected the psalms. Or else he might have probed the mysteries of creation. With God as his only company on the mountain he would have yearned to learn the secrets of His power. What drew up the sun from the well of night, who fathered the birds, and who had created the biped, at once so sturdy and fragile? Incredibly, he thought about none of this. He had only withdrawn from those slaves at the foot of the mountain so that he might return to them a better guide. Exhausted by the daily effort of keeping discipline in their ranks, he had realized that no single person could maintain order for anyone else. Unless these dissatisfied men and women began to assume greater responsibility for themselves and one another, they would either murder him in the desert and die there after him or else deteriorate as they watched him grow feeble. He had to absent himself temporarily from their squabbles and the smallness of their desires so as to conceive for them a dignified way of life.

Through all of this, it never occurred to him that his fate might be independent of theirs. Even the love he felt when he reached up to caress God's face in the heavens at night reminded him that he had yet to instil that love in His children down below. In stone, using the primitive implements at hand, he carved the laws on the tablets as he would have to inscribe them still more laboriously on their souls. One does not have to stand in awe of God; it is enough to stand in awe of Moses.

Anyway, our trip was not quite the same after that. Odd, how many conversations we entered into on the way down the mountain with people we hadn't previously spoken to at all. The two boys who had been trying to pick up the Harvard coed and had merged with her into a comradely threesome— it turned out that their fathers who ran small textile factories in Lyons came from Bialystok, as did my father who was also in textiles. I recognized from the Yiddish that they began speaking between themselves and teaching to Janie on the way down the mountain that their parents must have come from the same region of Poland–Lithuania as mine. We exchanged addresses, and a few weeks later my father actually received a letter from one of their parents, asking after lost relatives. And together, you and I discovered that our own *landsman* the French-Canadian from Trois Rivières was on the trip because of a book she had read on the Holocaust. She said that the purpose of her trip to Israel was to understand the Jews of whom Jesus had been one, and whose fate theirs so resembled. She had applied for a job as French teacher in a Montreal Jewish day school and meant to use the pictures she was busily snapping of the mountain as classroom material. I suggested that her students might benefit more from her intimate knowledge of Trois Rivières, but nothing could puncture her zeal.

Late that afternoon we made our most startling discovery. It was when we were sitting around in the long shadow of the trucks after the last stragglers had rejoined us. The guides had brought us a bag of dried fruit and nuts to pass around, and as you handed it to the person beside you he said "*todah*" ("thanks"). "*Ata medaber ivrit?*" ("You speak Hebrew?") you asked him unsteadily. "*Betakh*" ("Of course"), he replied, with an Hebrew accent more native than yours. He then began to explain to you that after arriving from Morocco with his family as a child, he had served here in the army—this man we knew only as the husband of Martine—and that he had brought his wife, her brother, and his sister-in-law on this outing to show them where he had been wounded in '67. We had passed the battle site on our way to the mountain the previous day. He had been hurt quite badly, and his reconstructed knee still gave him a bit of trouble. (Was it possible, then, that Martine's heels were a fond wife's ingenious camouflage for his handicap?) Now he lived on Rue Mozart in Paris, and in partnership with his brother-in-law ran a large store of children's clothing. In the summer he visited his family in Israel. It had been a mistake for Martine to attempt the climb in those unsuitable shoes, but the two women were intending to stay at the campsite, and had something unforeseen not occurred the night before they would never have set out. His wife had dreamt a strange dream. In her dream the stars had issued her an invitation to come up to the top of the mountain where Moïse had been given the Law, and in the morning she had refused to be left behind. His wife had a strong will. She had been raised in Morocco in the very religious household of her uncle and had memorized whole sections of the Torah, although she otherwise knew not a word of Hebrew. When they finally got to the top (after most of us had already begun our descent) his wife had declaimed for them the Ten Commandments.

I didn't hear most of this conversation as I was sitting quite a distance away from you, and people kept passing back and forth between us while you spoke with him. I don't recall either exactly what I felt when you told me about it that night. Surprise, certainly, and confusion. It occurred to me that the guides and some of us Hebrew speakers had said unpleasant things about them assuming that they could not understand us, and so without bothering to check whether they were out of earshot. Was Martine's husband impervious to insult, or had he pretended not to hear so as to protect his wife from the things that were being said about her? In a sense, their behavior was cast in an even more disturbing light by the knowledge that they considered themselves to be proud and self-conscious Jews. Evidently, the Jewish tribe had not been advanced as far as some of us had hoped through the

Epilogue: Reflections on Love and Loyalty

moral discipline of Sinai, or perhaps the discipline had been eroded through too many migrations and shocks of modernity? It was possible to believe that their tenuous loyalties to Jewish Law and family might eventually turn them into worthier people, or else to see in them the abject failure of Jewish civilization in the modern period.

As we scrambled to readjust our image of these fellow Jews our behavior, too, seemed more disturbing in retrospect. From the moment they joined our group, we enjoyed the relative goodness their misdeeds gave us the right to feel about ourselves. We allowed their carelessness to relax our standards by a notch or two even as it reinforced our self-righteousness. Assuming no familial responsibility for them, we were prepared to condemn what they did rather than trying as our brothers' keepers to improve them. Without for a moment excusing them, we might have done better to confront the barbarism (even if the guides did not) rather than waiting, like spectators, for The Plot to resolve itself.

As I say, I don't recall exactly how I felt when you told me of your conversation that night, but right now at this moment of trying to untangle my feelings, I'm tired. If you've read this letter through, you may be feeling likewise. It's the tiredness I recognize of moral battle fatigue, and it must be connected with all the many claims of duty that by now marshall the mind and soul. Just look at my perversity: a bolt of desire summons up the memory of you, and I sit down to write to you because I want to keep it momentarily alive. On paper at least, I want to recover what the loon has stirred up in me, only in the course of retrieving that stab of pleasure I spin out the very net of moral considerations that will entangle and finally trap me. Sex requires momentary suspension of moral disbelief. "And they gave themselves up utterly to love" must be attended by "And they saw that it was good." I am approaching the point in our narrative when we could no longer give ourselves up to love because we could no longer believe that it was good.

Are you smiling at my use of the plural pronoun? Don't worry. I am not suffering from loss of memory or resorting to poetic licence. It was you alone who decided that we would have to leave our love behind in the desert because it couldn't be adapted to the requirements of civilization. I fought you with every argument in my arsenal. You were the one who explained, and soothed me, and cajoled, and reassured me, and who finally convinced me not through any of your manifold powers of persuasion but because there was no way I could rape you, that is, have you against your will. You forced me to accept a decision you had reached on your own. Yet, having accepted the decision that you forced on me, am I not entitled to join you in it?

The beach at Dahab where we spent the last night was much rockier than the sandy terrain of the desert. I could feel the stones in my back through both sleeping bags, and I thought you were referring to that bruising pressure from the ground when you asked me, so uncharacteristically, "Am I hurting you?" Tears of pleasure sprung to my eyes at that marriage of your power within me and your solicitude over me. I wanted you to stay and to root yourself inside me like a tree, there in that inhospitable ground. But your question was deceptive, perhaps the only dishonesty of which I could ever accuse you. You were referring not to any pain of the moment—by that time you were at least as stone-pocked as I was—but to the terrible pain you were intending to inflict on me by ceasing, as soon as this final thrust was over, to "hurt" me ever again. You had decided that at the point of rejoining our spouses and resuming our regular lives we would have to become loving friends instead of lovers. We would have to abide by the seventh commandment. I would never feel the sweet rise of you inside me again.

Let me tell you what I've told you before. I could not have done what you did. The rest of that night and during most of the next day when you gave what may well have been the most inspired legal address of your life, you persuaded me that you were trying to keep us together rather than drive us apart. Whatever callow motives I ascribed to you, I came to believe that you were right. We were not Tristan or Isolde, after all, but someone else's husband and wife, and we would not be able to sustain for very long a tawdry double life. The pictures you drew—of us scurrying around the city to rendezvous in a hotel room between four and five in the afternoon and then later bumping into one another on parents' night in the high school where we both intended to send our children—they were realistic and ugly pictures. If adultery in an age of effective birth control skirted the biological hazards of earlier times, it still undeniably retained enough poisoning powers to destroy most of family loyalty and family life. Impossible to have to lie perpetually in answer to such simple questions as, where are you going, or, what did you do this afternoon, without deforming the basic trust of our two marriages. There was too much love in our young families to warrant undoing them for the promise of love between you and me, and that being the case, there was too much to risk in the permanent masquerade that a love affair would require.

I was startled when you even went so far as to invoke Judaism and its consideration of happiness as a standard for civilizing ourselves. That was probably the first time I heard anyone, that is, anyone of our generation, apply Judaism as a guide to right action. Having been raised without regard for the specific directives of Jewish law, I had come to regard Jewishness as a kind of innate idea of right action, one that, having been born an ethical Jew, I could presumably adjust indefinitely to my own desires. Suddenly, you were telling me that being a Jew meant accepting the discipline of a Jew; that the mountain we'd climbed for adventure was a place of true consequence.

Naturally, I've often suspected you of feeling a lesser degree of desire for me than I felt for you, of wanting to dump me for the sake of convenience, using morality for your excuse. But the attribution of motives to you is an exercise in solipsism, since I can never know your motives, even assuming that you could. Rejection is what most of us imbibed with our mother's milk, and we are as much attracted to it as we are to the nurturing love that was its accompaniment. The many times I rehearsed your "rejection" of me I was nursing some ancient deprivation that had little to do with you, although it was obviously important to me to believe that it issued from you. In the long run, what truly mattered was not your motive, but your words and the deeds that they confirmed. All those hundreds of times that we spoke on the phone or talked over coffee or lunch, I would have scrapped my "morals" with the same abandon that Martine lost the heel of

Epilogue: Reflections on Love and Loyalty

her shoe. Maybe knowing that made it easier for you to police us. Certainly, the laws of Sinai alone could never have disciplined me. What contained me finally was that you said no.

Improbably, you taught me loyalty, which God makes the basis of His covenant. The modern temper distrusts loyalty on many counts—psychologically, for breeding passivity; intellectually, for stifling creativity; socially, for encouraging conformity; politically, for fostering tyranny. The experimental modern temper finds in loyalty the comical foil to its own elasticity or the threatening challenge to its self-reliance. Intellectuals, especially, boast of their iconoclasm, and Jewish intellectuals may work the hardest of all to establish their independence from a collective association that makes great demands from within and exposes them to embarrassing assaults from without.

But I think the arguments you once mounted against adultery are also the basis of every other kind of discipline. The opposite of loyalty is disloyalty, a rotten quality, whatever attractive notions it holds of itself. Psychologically, it breeds selfishness; intellectually, it rewards lying; socially, it cultivates irresponsibility; politically, it invites tyranny. Although every rebel claims to be Prometheus defying the power of Zeus to bring warmth to humankind, or Spartacus, defying the power of Rome to bring freedom to slaves, these claims depend—don't they?—on the nature of the law that is being defied. When you belong to a people that upholds freedom above all, the opposition to its authority is really a blow against freedom. The French couples could not be punished for so flagrantly disobeying the rules and neither could we be stoned for our sin. Civilization today depends on our willingness to remain a part of it.

Well, my longing for you has this advantage at least: I shall never be effortlessly moral. I don't welcome exertion for its own sake, but we incipient sinners have a pungent appreciation of the fruits of the moral life. Maybe because I had to give up something precious for their sake, the simple lines of attachment that bind me to my husband and our children and friends and families become more precious with time. Not the least of my gains is that I've been able to love you unstintingly, just as you are, a family man. These may be staid pleasures compared to the thrills I sometimes crave, but they are generous pleasures that can be enjoyed shamelessly before all the world. They will have to suffice.

Notes

8 "The whole Arab people is unalterably opposed . . .": Evidence submitted by the Arab office, Jerusalem, to the Anglo-American Committee of Inquiry, March 1946. In *The Israel-Arab Reader*, edited by Walter Laqueur (Bantam Books, New York, 1969), pp. 94–104.

27 Nathan Glazer, *Affirmative Discrimination: Ethnic Inequality and Public Policy* (Basic Books, New York, 1975).

  Nathan Glazer, "Jews and American Liberalism," in *American Jewry: Dreams and Realities*, edited by Naomi W. Cohen, Norman J. Cohen, and Robert M. Seltzer (New York University Press, New York, 1993).

  Milton Himmelfarb, *The Jews of Modernity* (Jewish Publication Society, Philadelphia, 1973), contains a number of essays on the association of

Jews with liberalism and analyses of American liberal voting patterns since 1960.

28   Peter Steinfels, "American Jews Stand Firmly to the Left," *New York Times*, January 8, 1989, p. 7. Steinfels quotes findings of the Los Angeles poll.

31   Glazer, "Jews and American Liberalism."

32   Irving Kristol, "The Future of American Jewry," *Commentary*, August 1991, pp. 21–26.

38–39   Glazer, "Jews and American Liberalism."

42   Charles S. Liebman and Steven M. Cohen, *Two Worlds of Judaism* (Yale University Press, New Haven, 1990), pp. 99–122.

43   Raymond Aron's description of ideology, *The Opium of the Intellectuals*, translated by Terence Kilmartin (University Press of America, Lanham, MD, 1985).

48   "*I* am burdened with collective guilt . . .": Jean Amery, "Resentments," in *At the Mind's Limits: Contemplations by a Survivor on Auschwitz and Its Realities*, translated by Sidney Rosenfeld and Stella P. Rosenfeld (Schocken, New York, 1986), p. 75.

49   Jacob Katz, *From Prejudice to Destruction: Anti-Semitism 1700–1933* (Harvard University Press, Cambridge, MA, 1980).

51–52   August Bebel, Resolution on anti-Semitism at the

Berlin Congress of the Social Democratic Party,
1893, quoted by Robert S. Wistrich in *Socialism
and the Jews* (Oxford University Press, New York,
1982), p. 133.

65   Robert S. Wistrich, *Revolutionary Jews; from
Marx to Trotsky* (Harrap, London, 1976).

71   Moses Hess, *Rome and Jerusalem,* translated by
Meyer Waxman (Bloch Publishing Co., New
York, 1945). All quotations from this source.

73   Isaiah Berlin, "The Life and Opinions of Moses
Hess," in *Against the Current: Essays in the
History of Ideas* (Hogarth Press, London, 1980),
p. 247.

110   Hillel Halkin, *Letters to an American Jewish
Friend* (Jewish Publication Society, Philadelphia,
1977), p. 18.

113–114 *The Diary of Anne Frank: The Critical Edition*
(Doubleday, Garden City, NY, 1986), pp. 600–
601.

120–121 Eugene V. Rostow, "The West Bank and the
Gaza Strip in International Law," *Middle East:
Uncovering the Myths* (Anti-Defamation League,
New York, 1991), pp. 28–29.

123   *New York Times,* March 24, 1989, p. 1.

125   "De Gaulle need an opportunity to distance
himself . . .": Henry H. Weinberg, *The Myth of
the Jew in France 1967–1982* (Mosaic Press,
Cincinnatti, OH, 1987), chap. 1.

126   Raymond Aron, *De Gaulle, Israel and the Jews*, translated by John Sturrock (Frederick A. Praeger, New York, 1969), p. 24.

136   Jean-François Revel, *How Democracies Perish*, translated by William Byron (Doubleday, Garden City, NY, 1983). Quotation on pp. 3–4.

144   Jean-Paul Sartre, *Anti-Semite and Jew*, translated by George J. Becker (Schocken, New York, 1948).

146   Batya Goor, *A Saturday Morning Murder* (in Hebrew) (Keter, Jerusalem, 1988).

150   S. Yizhar, "The Prisoner," translated by V. C. Rycus in *Israeli Stories*, edited by Joel Blocker (Schocken, New York, 1965), pp. 152–174. Quotation on pp. 158–159.

153   "I feel that to the great boons . . .": Henry Roth's contribution to *Midstream* symposium on "The Meaning of *Galut* in America Today," March 1963, p. 33.

156   A. B. Yehoshua, "Facing the Forests," translated by Miriam Arad in *Modern Hebrew Literature*, edited by Robert Alter (Behrman House, West Orange, NJ, 1975), pp. 357–392. Quotation on p. 387.

161   Franz Kafka, *The Trial*, translated by Willa and Edwin Muir (Schocken, New York, 1946). The first German edition based on Kafka's manuscripts was published in 1925; a revised edition in 1935.

163   Isaac Babel, "Argamak" translated by Andrew R.
       MacAndrew, in *Lyuba the Cossack and Other
       Stories* (Signet, New York, 1963), p. 150.

164   Amos Oz, *In the Land of Israel*, translated by
       Maurice Goldberg-Bartura (Harcourt Brace Jo-
       vanovich, New York, 1983), p. 163.

165–166 David Grossman, *The Yellow Wind*, translated by
       Haim Watzman (Farrar, Straus and Giroux, New
       York, 1988). Quotation from p. 7.

169   Gabi Daniel (pseudonym), "Peter hagadol," in
       Igra: Almanac for Literature and Art, edited by
       Dan Miron and Natan Zach (Keter, Jerusalem,
       1985–86), pp. 199–200.

Printed in the United States
By Bookmasters